Praise for *No Mission No Margin*

"No Mission No Margin *is a must read for those who are new to hospice governance and management and Patti Moore is the perfect person to write it. A hospice pioneer, she was a successful hospice provider. As a member of hospice leadership organizations she helped shape the evolution of care delivery in her state and our nation. As a consultant she has been exposed to the wide variety of problems and opportunities hospices have encountered, regardless of profit status. Most importantly, she understands first-hand the tensions that exist when clinicians, managing death as a complex human event, encounter reimbursement regulations that largely recognize it as a medical one. Patti takes a strong position that it is simply not enough to care about the dying and those who care for them. The care, and the organization's management, must be done competently, with a respectful appreciation for the roles of regulation, education and philanthropy. When this is done well, studies show patients not only die more comfortably, but there is a significant chance that some will live longer than those who have not received hospice."*

– TRUE RYNDES, ANP, MPH
Recipient of the National Hospice and Palliative Care Organization's Founders Award and author

To Christine,
Many Blessings,
Patti Moore

NO
MISSION
NO
MARGIN

Creating a Successful Hospice
with Care and Competence

NO
MISSION
NO
MARGIN

PATRICE C. MOORE
RN, BSN, MSN, ARNP

Advantage®

Published by Advantage, Charleston, South Carolina.
Member of Advantage Media Group.

ADVANTAGE is a registered trademark and the Advantage colophon is a trademark of Advantage Media Group, Inc.

Printed in the United States of America.

ISBN: 978-1-59932-467-8
LCCN: 2014954032

This publication is designed to provide accurate and authoritative information in regard to the subject matter covered. It is sold with the understanding that the publisher is not engaged in rendering legal, accounting, or other professional services. If legal advice or other expert assistance is required, the services of a competent professional person should be sought.

Advantage Media Group is proud to be a part of the Tree Neutral® program. Tree Neutral offsets the number of trees consumed in the production and printing of this book by taking proactive steps such as planting trees in direct proportion to the number of trees used to print books. To learn more about Tree Neutral, please visit **www.treeneutral.com**. To learn more about Advantage's commitment to being a responsible steward of the environment, please visit **www.advantagefamily.com/green**

Advantage Media Group is a publisher of business, self-improvement, and professional development books and online learning. We help entrepreneurs, business leaders, and professionals share their Stories, Passion, and Knowledge to help others Learn & Grow. Do you have a manuscript or book idea that you would like us to consider for publishing? Please visit **advantagefamily.com** or call **1.866.775.1696**.

To my beloved Stephen,

With profound appreciation for your unwavering love
and encouragement; Your strength has given me
the courage to realize my dreams.

---

*"Being deeply loved by someone gives you strength,
while loving someone deeply gives you courage."*

LAO TZU

Table of Contents

 I n t r o d u c t i o n

"The problems of the world can't be solved by skeptics or cynics whose horizons are limited by the obvious realities. We need men who can dream things that never were."

—JOHN FITZGERALD KENNEDY

"We pay the same whether the care is good or whether it is not good. The current sector is all about volume. The future is about value."

—MICHAEL LEAVITT, FORMER SECRETARY OF HEALTH AND HUMAN SERVICES

The looming changes in our health-care system brought by the Affordable Care Act will be the most impactful since the 1960s and the creation of Medicare. As of this writing, no one knows how it will ultimately unfold, but the quote above from Michael Leavitt provides us with a hint.

Historically, health care has worked through payment for services rendered: health-care providers submitted their charges and were paid for care given. The more services they provided, the more they were paid. However, limits began to be placed on what could and could not be provided as insurance companies became increasingly specific about what they would and would not cover. Generally, Medicare paid for treatments regardless of outcome, which is part of the reason we have seen the costs of health care burgeon, and why cost/outcome ratios are inferior to those in other countries. According to the World Health Organization (WHO), the United States spends a higher portion of its gross domestic product on health care, annually, than any other country. Yet, the United States ranks 37th out of 191 countries in the WHO's ranking of health-care systems.

The intent of the Affordable Care Act is to transform our illness-based health-care paradigm to focusing more on prevention and healthy communities and to put care within reach of more people for whom it was previously unaffordable. What that will do for hospice is uncertain at this time, but hospice will be impacted. At a minimum, it will intensify the demand for accountability, quality, and performance, requiring hospices to ensure that what they say they are going to do, they *actually* do. We will likely see increasing emphasis on partnering with other health-care players to improve the patient's experience.

Hospice has never been a high-cost part of our health-care expenditure; it has actually saved money. Hospice patients are more likely to spend the last 60 days of their life at home, not in a hospital where they are subjected to futile treatments that probably will not make a difference in their outcome. This results in more savings of health-care dollars but also, and more importantly, it allows for more appropriate care in the patients' preferred setting.

To understand where hospice is today, we need to look at how it began. Prior to the 1970s there were not many options for people who had cancer or chronic illnesses. They would be admitted to the hospital, sometimes staying there for long periods of time, where their pain could be managed, usually by injections or intravenous medications. There were few attempts to get into the existential examination of life and death. Health care was about the treatment of disease. If you could be made well, that was great. If not, comfort measures were few.

In London, England, in the 1960s, Cicely Saunders (made a dame of the British Empire in 1989) worked her way up through the health-care system, starting out as a nurse and then becoming a social worker and finally, a physician. Having seen patient care from multiple perspectives, she felt there must be something more that could be done for people at the end of life. Often she found people who were dying in hospitals were simply put at the end of the long halls because "there was nothing more that could be done." One of her terminal patients left her a small legacy to create a special place of care for dying people and their loved ones. Dame Cicely started the first modern-day hospice in London in 1967 and named it St. Christopher's. It was a place where people could go and stay until they died. They were treated like a whole person rather than someone with a disease. They could wear their own clothes and eat when and what they wanted, and their families and pets could visit at any time. Dame Cicely believed there was much more that could be done for the dying. It was a revolutionary idea that quickly caught on.

Meanwhile, in 1969, in the United States, Dr. Elisabeth Kubler-Ross published her ground-breaking book *On Death and Dying* for which she interviewed 500 terminally ill patients about their experiences. What she heard convinced her that much more needed to be done for the dying than simply giving them a shot for pain while ignoring all the other pieces of our common human experience as we face the greatest journey in life, the journey of death. A grassroots movement of people across the

United States—nurses, physicians, ministers, social workers, and lay people—began to volunteer to shape an Americanized version of hospice care for people at the end of life. This groundswell of revolutionaries began meeting in church basements, living rooms, and hospital conference rooms to come up with better models of care for the dying. The first hospice in the United States was established in Connecticut in 1974, patterned after the one in England. The United States is so expansive that a single hospice facility was not a practical way to serve such a scattered population, so the home-based American hospice model was formed.

This voluntary hospice movement began as a way of saying, "We are going to care for people in a new way. We are going to respect people who are dying, not just as people with a terminal illness but as human beings who have spiritual, social, and emotional needs, and their loved ones who are also impacted by their death." Hospice care developed with the aim of empowering patients to take charge of how they wished to live until the moment of death.

The first National Hospice Conference took place in 1979 in St. Louis. In 1982 the US Congress included a provision to create a Medicare hospice benefit allowing Medicare to pay for hospice care for people who had six months or less to live. That major adjustment to Medicare was championed by a bipartisan group of Congressmen. They were persuaded by relatives of those who had suffered in traditional care, by hospice workers and faith-based groups, by health-care workers, and by all those whose eyes had been opened by Dr. Kubler-Ross's book and Dame Cicely's hospice in London.

Following World War II, public hospitals increasingly became the places where people would go to receive care and, if necessary, stay until death. But many who were facing the end of their lives wanted to be at home, not in a hospital. Hospice care generally consists of physical, emotional, spiritual, and social care. It is not just the patient who's receiving care; the patient and the family are the "unit of care." Nurses, social workers/counselors, doctors, nursing aides, and volunteers are all involved.

The Medicare hospice benefit, approved by the US Congress in 1982, is brilliant because it focuses on caring for people in a holistic way and allows people who are dying to tailor the hospice benefit to fit their particular needs. Some patients may need a nurse to help with pain management. Others may need more time with a social worker for counseling or guidance on financial or community resources, while still others may want spiritual care and the opportunity to talk about the meaning of life and what their legacy will be. The beauty of hospice care is that, ideally, it can offer all of those things.

Hospices across the United States have interpreted the Medicare benefit in broad and narrow ways. There are a variety of models of hospice care: the not-for-profit, community-based hospices that care for tens of thousands of patients a day offer extreme levels of community involvement, not just the required core components. Some hospices have board-certified medical care, pastoral care from CPE trained chaplains, social workers/counselors with master's degrees, and hundreds of volunteers, and unique services such as pediatric care, children's grief camps, veteran's programs, music therapy, massage therapy, Reiki, aromatherapy, and even pet therapy. Alternatively, there are very small programs that offer just the basics of care by a nurse, a physician, a volunteer, and/or social worker, and/or a chaplain. There are also enormous, national, for-profit hospice companies that serve patients across the United States in multiple communities and states. Hospice services vary greatly across the country.

I have been working in hospice care for 30 years. In retrospect, it seems it was preordained: My dad was a fire-fighter and my mother was a homemaker and hairdresser. Caring for other people was what we did in our family. I always wanted to be in a helping profession, and I loved science and anatomy, so becoming a nurse was a natural choice. I went to the community college, got my AA degree in science and microbiology, and then went to the University of Florida and received a bachelors and later a masters degree in nursing.

I had never had anyone close to me die, but in 1976, I attended a lecture by Cicely Saunders who had come to Orlando to talk about hospice, and I was tremendously inspired.

I began in 1983 as an executive director of a tiny hospital-based hospice in Gainesville, Florida. Our office was a remodeled elevator shaft, a windowless space with walls that were two feet thick. When I started, we had three staff members, two of whom worked part-time, 15 volunteers, and five patients. We didn't charge fees; it was a free service offered by our community hospital, Alachua General. It came about through a coalition of the community's ministers, physicians, volunteers, hospital auxiliary ladies, and the chief executive officer (CEO) of the hospital, who had agreed to sponsor this innovation. Our annual budget was $50,000. We created the rules as we went along and we were advocates for public policy in Tallahassee to make sure Florida had a hospice licensure law so there would be a standard of hospice care in our state.

We cared for people as if they were our family members. We were on call 24 hours a day, seven days a week. We stood with people who were dying and were their advocates. We trained physicians to be brave enough to order narcotics in large doses to manage people's pain. We developed the state association, Florida Hospices, Inc., through which we all shared with one another policies and procedures and frameworks of how to provided loving hospice care.

It was a privilege to have been a part of that initial movement because we changed the way people were cared for at the end of their life. And healing took place, not always in the sense of getting better and continuing to live for long periods of time but in the sense of spiritual healing. We saw patients and families change before our eyes when pain was relieved or long-standing feuds were resolved. It was the most amazing and profound work I had ever done.

The word *hospice* is derived from the Latin root meaning *hospitality*. The original idea started in the Middle Ages, along crusade trails where people would offer way-stations for weary travelers as they made their way across Europe. Now, here we are, 1,000 years later, helping people on their final journey of life, standing with them, offering them comfort, encouragement, listening to their fears, listening to their dreams, listening to their hopes, and helping them to make as much of life as possible.

I was the executive director for almost 16 years, and by the time I left, we had cared for 270 patients a day across 11 counties in north central Florida. We had approximately 190 employees and 450 volunteers, and we had built an 18-bed hospice care center. We were making a meaningful difference in the way people were cared for, and I was proud of my contributions. I wanted to continue to challenge myself, to take the not-for-profit community model of care that I'd seen work so brilliantly in Gainesville and share that with people around the country. So I started my own consulting business in 1999. I named it The Watershed Group because, metaphorically, a watershed moment is a turning point. I was at a turning point in my life. I knew there would be organizations and people who would arrive at their own watershed moments and need someone to help them through, and I wanted to be that guide.

As founder and president of The Watershed Group, I have worked with people all over the country. It was the life and early death of my brother Michael that inspired and empowered me to start my company. Michael had lived his life exactly the way he wanted to live it. Instead of working for someone else, he created a business. When he died, I thought that if he could do it, I could too. My purpose is to help those people who are dying and the people who love them have the best life experience they can. That's what drives me; even though I might be three or more degrees of separation from patients, I never forget that fact.

Why am I writing this book now? I started my business because I wanted to take what I knew to be true and share it with those in the field who are looking for inspiration and encouragement. Over the last 30 years I have seen the hospice movement go from its humble beginnings on the fringes of health care to the mainstream. Over the last five or six years, I have seen growing concerns about the financial challenges and cutbacks: How are we going to do more with less? I have seen finances became a big focal point for hospices struggling to survive.

I am writing this book to remind people that, in the end, it is about the mission of hospice care. If you can stay true to the mission of caring for people at the end of their lives and supporting their desires, the rest will follow. You have seen books based on the theme of "do what you love and the money will follow." It is the same with hospice work. Never forget that your main job is easing the pain and suffering of the dying and their families; keep that first and foremost on your mind and let the rest of it flow. It is not easy, but by focusing on the mission, which includes balancing the margin, you will succeed.

We now have patients with new needs. We have a new health-care system, and perhaps a new payment system. As we move forward, we need to take the best of what we have learned and build on that. This book is to help hospice managers, leaders, and board members remember why they are doing this work, and to give them some tools to do the best work that they can for dying patients and their families and their communities.

Chapter One

"Without a sense of caring, there can be no sense of community."

—ANTHONY J. D'ANGELO

CREATING A CULTURE OF CARE

The idea of great care is central to any successful business, particularly hospice. From the Chief Executive Officer/Executive Director (CEO/ED) to the volunteers serving the patients, excellent care must stay central to what we do. What are the nuts and bolts of creating a corporate culture that supports that mission? It is useful to be reminded of the *why* of the work. Always ask, "Why are we doing this work?" Hopefully, the answer is because you love what you do and you want to make a difference in someone else's life. Certainly, in hospice, the mission is very noble. It's easier to find meaning in the work of caring for people who are facing the end of their life, and their loved ones, than it might be in most other work.

When I work with boards of directors or senior leadership teams who want to talk about strategy or the future, I always start with mission-centered questions such as: What are your core values? What is it that makes you want to do this work? Why do you think you are doing something that is unique or special? What is it that you believe you can do better than anyone else? I often ask people to identify the top five words that, for them, express their values related to this work. If they could take everything else away, what would be those top three or five words that represent the *why* of the work they do?

Sometimes, those words include *integrity, caring, love,* or *service.* Your focus on those words is the kernel from which everything else grows and that will dictate the framework of how you run your hospice. Values and vision and belief are all key parts of that framework. As a leader, you set the tone, and it is up to you to surround yourself with people who share those same values, so that you can be sure they are all working from the same viewpoint. I believe you have to deeply care about the people with whom you work because if you only care about your own image, or about the bottom line and meeting the numbers, you lose touch with the people who go out to deliver patient care regardless of the setting. They are your hospice. They are the ones who make a difference in the lives of dying people. They are your brand.

Creating a culture of care means respecting all of the people with whom you work, from the housekeeper to the doctor, because they are all integral to the work that's being done. Everyone has something to contribute. Being the CEO/ED does not necessarily mean you are the smartest person in the organization, or have all the answers. Including people in the mission of the work, asking them for their input, and giving them honest feedback are all very important parts of creating culture and essential for the success of any organization.

I read an interesting article in the Delta Airlines in-flight magazine recently. Delta CEO Richard Anderson said, "At Delta, we have found that common values are far better than any detailed manual could ever be. When you're flying 150 million people a year around the globe, there are too many variables to write rules for. Delta people, from the CEO's office to the front lines, rely on our culture and our core values to guide our business decisions every day. Sure, we have rules, but our values help us know when the rules are sufficient. Bending the rules, especially for our most loyal customers, is often just the right thing to do." Here is the CEO of one of the top global companies, with thousands of employees, talking about the culture that they have created, their core values, and how that informs their work. Hospices too must never lose sight of their core values. Many decisions have to be made on an individual basis, and a strong culture of understanding how far you can go and where you need to stop is essential.

CRAFTING THE MISSION STATEMENT

Every hospice needs a mission statement, but the problem with mission statements is that too often they are written with great intentions and then framed on a wall and never looked at again.

Your mission statement should be your North Star, your guide when you find yourself lost in the woods. It needs to start with the board of directors because that is the group that is ultimately responsible for your organization, whether the hospice is a not-for-profit or for-profit. The crafting of a meaningful, functional mission statement begins with identifying those values-based words that describe what is important in what you do, and then identifying the top five or six words that you cannot live without.

The next thing that needs to be addressed is why your organization exists. Do you simply want to help hospice-eligible patients who are dying or do you serve chronically ill people as well? Do you want to educate the community? How far do you want to take your mission? Some hospice boards are focused narrowly on hospice care in their own communities only, and are not interested in contributing to the greater good. You must decide how broad or narrow the focus of your organization will be.

Once the board has agreed upon the mission, gather representatives from throughout the organization, from the home health aides, the housekeepers, and the clerical people to the nurses and the social workers, the doctors, and the chaplains, and form an advisory committee whose function it is to look critically at how that mission gets put into play, how it informs everyone's work on a day-to-day basis, and how it is taken from statement to fact. The mission statement has to be a dynamic document, not simply something that is crafted in an executive meeting and then handed down as law.

Your mission statement needs to be kept at the forefront of the decision-making process. Every time you have a meeting and there is a question about the organization's direction, consult it. Does the new direction fit into your mission? An example of that might be when someone on your team wants something that is outside the Medicare benefit but it seems like the right thing to do because, as your mission statement claims, "We care for people, regardless of their ability to pay." If you believe that, then how far do you take that? Subsequently, every executive meeting, board meeting, and interdisciplinary team meeting should begin with a story that reflects that mission. A report on what happened in the field during the previous week should be delivered along with an example of how you and your colleagues put the hospice mission into action.

An unexpected kindness, care given over and above the standard, the funeral service the chaplain performed for the patient who had no one else—those are the things that keep people passionate about this work. We all need to be reminded that living the mission is more important than creating a mission statement. As leaders, you have to empower and trust your people to interpret those rules as they will. The example of Delta is a good one because it underlines the fact that the bottom line for Delta's corporate culture is doing the best it can for its customers even though that may not mean the same thing in every instance. The important thing to remember is that if an action is taken in the spirit of meeting the mission and the hospice's core values, it is the right thing to do.

EMPOWERING THE PATIENT

Hospice work began with general ideas of care rather than strict rules. We simply supported people by giving them the information they needed to make informed decisions about their own care, about how they wanted to live their lives at the end of life. It was aimed at helping people realize they could be comfortable and pain-free, they could say no to a treatment or an intervention, or they could say yes to a surgery or an alternative type of care. It was less about the rules and regulations of hospice and more about the bigger question my friend and hospice pioneer Mary Labyak, former CEO of Suncoast Hospice, would always ask: "What do you want for the rest of your life and how can we help you achieve that?"

When Medicare began to pay for hospice, more formal rules were instituted. Soon, the Medicare benefit and states licensure laws began dictating the regulations for hospice care. In some cases, we have drifted so far from the beginnings of hospice that some hospice programs simply list, as their services, the rules of the Medicare hospice benefit. For care to be paid by Medicare, we are required to adhere to a minimum set of standards, but hospices should be more than that. Instead of hospice staff asking, "What kind of insurance do you have?" or saying, "No, we don't offer that," staff at a true, community-based hospice must ensure the patient's desires are met. Perhaps those desires include having a volunteer read to you often, or having the social worker arrange for someone to prepare your will or a statement that you want to share with your family members. Maybe you want the counselor to support the children in the family with play therapy, or the physician to make visits to the home to support the care system in place, or you want to go into the hospice facility for respite care. Whatever the need, we need to strive to find a way in which to fill it.

Avow Hospice in Naples, Florida cared for a woman in her 30s with two young children. As she was dying she was worried that her children would not remember her. The nurse manager asked the IT director to find a way to videotape an interview with her. They set up the interview, and the mother told her children the things she wanted them to know and how much she loved them.

The nurse who told me the story said that she ran into the woman's husband several years after the woman died, and he said, "You have no idea what you did for my children. They watch the video of their mother almost every day, and that meant more to us than anything else." Sometimes, we need to be able to offer people what they most want, which could be things far beyond the Medicare hospice benefit.

Sometimes the services people need are the simple things. People need their pain relieved before they can do anything else, but once they are pain-free, hospice staff can begin to help them find meaning in this last phase of human existence. In this country, death is something we push away as hard as we can. We stage crusades against disease: the war on cancer, the war on heart disease. We fight against death at all costs. We subject ourselves to all kinds of treatments and surgeries because we want one last chance at life, but at some point we need to realize that living a good life does not mean escaping death. None of us do. Those of us working in hospice need to help the dying understand that instead of fighting against the inevitable, embracing the time they have left may be the best thing they can do. Yet, hospice care is not about preventing patients from having treatment. It is, rather, about understanding what their wishes are and supporting them.

My friend Becky McDonald, one of the pioneer hospice leaders in the United States, was diagnosed with lung cancer. Having suffered through a devastating round of chemotherapy that nearly killed her, she told her doctor she wanted to stop the treatment. He suggested she try it for another month, but she said, "I want to be able to be with my grandchildren and my children when I am feeling well. I don't want them coming to my bedside when I cannot touch them, hold them, or care for them. If it means I have one less month to live and I can do it with more energy, then that is what I want to do."

Allowing people to have those kinds of choices is empowering. When people enter a hospice, they are usually unaware of all that is available to them because they are not interested in learning about hospice care until they have to. We can help people realize what their choices are at the end of life and give them back as much power as possible to live out their lives as fully possible. When we hear a family member say, "I'm so proud of the care we gave our loved one," then, as hospice workers, we should be delighted because we empowered them to do it themselves. It is not about us taking over. It is not about us swooping in, saying, "I'm the expert. Step aside; we are taking over now." It is about asking, "What is it you want for your life? Let us help you achieve those goals."

It frustrates me to hear about hospice staff who say to patients: "This is what you have to do." I once worked with a hospice whose patients' wife wanted to crawl into her husband's bed at the nursing home to comfort him, but the facility nurse told her, "Oh, no. You're going to disturb him. You can't do that." The woman was understandably distraught because she had been married for 65 years and that was the currency of their relationship: she comforted him and he comforted her, and that embrace was far more important than what the nurse thought the patient needed. Our work is about what *they* want, not our expectations of a good death.

CREATING THE CULTURE OF CARE

How do we create a culture of care? I recently worked with an organization that had a very autocratic leader who didn't really want to know what the staff thought or cared about; he just wanted them to do their jobs. He was all about the bottom line. How does staff respond to a leader who only focuses on the numbers and not on the mission of care? Creating your corporate culture is where you have to start, which like the Disney culture begins with first caring for one another, and then for customers.

Part of that caring is sharing information with the staff about the nuts and bolts of running the hospice, starting with how you budget. I would always tell staff, "Budgeting here is just like your checkbook at home. We have a limited number of dollars, and we need to know where we can spend and where we need to save." I believe that helping the staff to understand how much things cost and what our expectations are helps them to be better stewards of the dollars that we are given from Medicare and Medicaid, private insurance, and donations.

All staff members should know how many patients the organization is serving each day—the average daily census— because there should be an understanding of the breakeven point. For example, if they are caring for 100 patients, they know there must be a certain number of staff to care for those patients, and if they have fewer patients than that, staffing should make adjustments.

Certainly, staffing is the largest expense on the balance sheet. The National Hospice and Palliative Care Organization (NHPCO) has guidelines for staff/patient ratios: One nurse can care for 12 to 15 patients; one social worker, for 35 to 40 patients; one chaplain, for 40 to 60 patients. Having those kinds of guidelines creates accountabilities so staff members understand that if the census goes down, they'll either need to help out somewhere else or take time off. Everybody needs to understand that we are all in this together. Certainly, the CEO/ED is the leader and has to be the one who oversees the budget, but if everyone recognizes what the costs are and that money allows us to carry out the mission of what we do, the result is a more empowered workforce in which we all know where we stand.

Medications are something that the Medicare hospice benefit requires the hospice to provide to dying patients. For instance, an order for a 14-day supply of morphine should be reduced to a supply for three to five days when it is clear that the patient may not live for more than a few days. Medication formularies can be put into place with guidelines on types of medications allowed, generic versus brand names, frequency of ordering, and so forth. Having guidelines in place helps staff, and the organization, ensure the best care at the best cost.

It's equally important to have clarity on what kind of core business you want to offer. Every hospice should be a good steward of the dollars it receives whether from the government, private payers, or community donations. It is the board of directors' responsibility to decide what type of financial performance is expected. It is the leadership team's responsibility to achieve that result.

Large hospice programs with a mission to impact the entire community on the topic of end-of-life care may decide to raise money to fund some of the unfunded programs such as enhanced bereavement programs for the entire community, children's programs, palliative and/or transitional care, and more. It is the board of directors who must agree that these are important programs for their community.

There are boards of directors who say, "At the end of the day, we want to have a positive margin, so we are going to run as lean as we can with staffing and other expenses because that's our mission." You must make sure that all the people who work for you know what your hospice's mission is, and how that mission is expected to be put into action.

As the dollars in health care continue to shrink, it is important that you accurately weigh what your community really wants and will support. Core hospice service must be provided by any hospice accepting Medicare funding. For anything beyond that, the board of directors and leadership staff must decide what to offer, what to raise money for, and what to discard because it is no longer important to users. Regularly ask the question: "Is this program still working or do we need something else?" Our hospice patient population is transitioning from the greatest generation to the baby boom generation, and they are going to want different services than their parents or their grandparents did. We should be asking them what they want and planning to help them achieve it, not just providing something because 10 or 15 years ago a staff member liked to do a particular program. Make sure what you are doing now still fits the needs of your community.

NO MARGIN, NO MISSION

The phrase "no margin, no mission" is attributed to Sister Irene Kraus of the Daughters of Charity. She was chief executive of the order's National Health System. She ran 36 hospitals and 19 other facilities in 17 states and was the first to chair the American Hospital Association. As a nun running a Catholic charity, mission was paramount, but she also understood that if you don't have the money to carry out your mission, your mission is unattainable. This has become the mantra in not-for-profit health care settings, because it is absolutely true: if you pay no attention to the financial side of things, you will soon be out of business. In the last decade, margin has sometimes taken on a greater emphasis than mission, making it even more crucial that we don't lose touch with our mission.

Betsy Gornet, Chief Advanced Illness Management Executive at Sutter Health, did her master's thesis on how not-for-profit hospital boards of directors function during crisis. She discovered that the most successful boards were those that had a balanced view of finances, quality, compliance, patient care, and marketing. Achieving that balance equals success. If you only focus on the margin, you're going to lose sight of the quality of care that's provided. By the same token, if you only focus on the care and don't concern yourself with the finances, the structure will topple.

Clearly, you must have accountability. Sometimes, compassionate cultures have difficulty in holding people accountable. Hospice organizations must collect their key data points and, in part, manage with them. The staff too must understand what the financial markers and data mean and be held accountable for their job performance in a compassionate manner. It is the job of the CEO/ED to make sure their organization exists for the future, and they must do what needs to be done to ensure that sustainability—all within the mission.

I was sitting on a plane out of Orlando one day when I had a conversation with the man seated next to me. Talk turned to our respective careers. I was surprised to hear that he ran the largest professional wrestling federation in the country. He'd been in Orlando filming matches and was returning home. Needless to say, I don't often meet people in that line of work. I asked him, "What do you think the most important thing has been for your success in this wrestling federation?"

He thought for a minute and then said, "It's about caring. I care about those guys who wrestle, and I care about their families, and they know that. So, they want to perform even better because they know I care." He added, "It doesn't mean I am not hard on them. In fact, there's somebody in the back of the plane that I have had to let go because he wasn't doing his job. It was hard for me, but he knew and I knew that if I didn't hold him accountable, everyone else would see that they didn't have to be accountable either."

I admit I was surprised. What were the chances that a professional wrestling federation CEO would talk about "care" being central to the success of that organization? But it is true. You must care and also hold people accountable. They will understand their own responsibility in a more meaningful way when both care and accountability are present.

STAYING CONNECTED

Whether it is through daily texts, weekly communications e-mails, staff meetings, workshops, retreats, or some other shared experience, it's vital to remind everyone, on a regular basis, how important they are to the work and how much they are appreciated. Remind them too of why this work matters. It is not something that can be shared just once, any more than you can tell someone you love him or her once and expect that to last a lifetime. This work we do is our job, but it impacts the quality of the lives of the people we serve, and we only have one chance to get it right for them. If we are not doing our best every single time, then someone is going to have an experience that will be less than what it should be. That is why it is crucial we remind staff that while we are concerned with how much things cost or how health-care reform is changing the way we are going to be paid, we have the unique privilege of being invited into people's lives, at the end of their lives, to walk with them on that journey, and we should never take that for granted.

We also must take care of ourselves. Hospice staff must not visit patients if they are overwhelmed by their own troubles or unable to be fully present with the person who is dying.

The more that leadership can communicate with front line staff, the better. Daily quotes of news and encouragement, weekly/ monthly internal blogs/newsletters about what is happening in the organization, and/or announcing weddings, births, graduations, and achievements of staff, all serve to bring people together as a community. Arrange for local volunteers and/or vendors to provide a day of pampering to the staff. Allowing time for laughter and sharing is powerful. It is also important to offer management staff the opportunity of an annual retreat to renew the values and mission of the organization.

Offering all staff reminders of the history of their organization, and where they fit into it, can enhance the culture. I recently did a workshop for a hospice organization entitled "Traditions," where in part we talked about the beginnings of their hospice. Who was the founder? What commitment and dedication did it take to get their hospice started? Are we still living those values? In addition to the things we typically use as yardsticks, such as the census, the length of stay, the referrals, admissions, discharges, revocations, and documentation, we must examine the culture and ensure it remains true to the original mission. Reviewing thank-you letters and complaints can help determine how we can improve our customers' experiences.

The big question is always: Is our culture still on track in our mission? How can we get to know each other better in order to make sure the trust we have with one another is strong, the respect we have for one another is high, and the engagement that we have with our patients and families is at a level we can be proud of?

A successful staff retreat or workshop of having fun together, sharing a meal together, and learning about each other as human beings outside our work improves trust. Many staff are responsible for the care of elder parents, kids, or ailing spouses at home. How do they manage that responsibility and then take care of 15 or 20 other people who are dying? Equipping staff with tools to make sure they take care of themselves is representative of a high performing organization.

Creating a powerful culture starts with appropriate hiring then connecting with staff as human beings. We must stay in touch with that soul part of ourselves and with our colleagues if we are to find the strength and commitment it takes to serve the mission of our work. There are so few people with the courage to stand next to someone who is dying and not flinch. It is imperative that we support those courageous souls who do. Whether it's via a luncheon, a staff meeting, a retreat, a workshop, or some other off-campus, out-of-the-ordinary shared activity, make the commitment to reconnect and recharge together. Support your staff while holding them accountable to do their jobs.

Chapter Two

"You become what you focus on and who you spend time with."

—PATRICE MOORE

HOSPICE IN TRANSITION

When hospice care began, some 40 years ago, it was the alternative to traditional care, an upstart movement. Over time, we have effected tremendous change nationally. Hospice went from being a marginal notion to being part of the Medicare health-care system, a remarkable shift. The Medicare hospice benefit was created in a bipartisan way, with leaders on both sides of the political aisle who believed this was good for all Americans.

Like all organizations, hospices have a life cycle. The original founders of hospice started out as entrepreneurs, with no rules in place, making it up as they went, with fire in their bellies to change the status quo. As that trajectory progressed into a more mature business, they had to apply more rules and regulations. They had to develop concrete policies and procedures, frameworks for growth and stability. When money became involved, checks and balances were implemented. Now we find ourselves at a point in hospice care where benefits are more narrowly defined and audits and investigations are the norm. Since the early years, people have interpreted the Medicare hospice benefit in many ways, offering a broad spectrum of services running from expanded types of care to very narrow interpretations of hospice care.

As more patients were admitted and Medicare expenditures for hospices increased, more scrutiny developed. The US Department of Health and Human Service's Office of the Inspector General began auditing hospice as well as many other health-care entities for potential fraud. Patients are eligible to elect hospice care if their physicians and the hospice physician certify that the patient is terminally ill, with a prognosis of six months or less if the disease runs its normal course. Estimating a person's length of life is not an exact science. Sometimes patients will live longer than their medical situation might suggest.

Organizations that started out as entrepreneurial were obliged to become increasingly more rigid in their attention to documentation, policies, and interpretation of the rules and regulations. This has made hospices less nimble or adaptable to what the market demands.

Another result of the increased focus on regulations has been the emergence of a different type of leader today than we saw 30 years ago. Originally, hospice leaders had to be inventive and creative, more likely to make the rules than to rigidly follow them. That generally led to more flexibility and creativity in hospice organizations. Today hospice leaders must adapt to increased scrutiny while their census may be declining, and manage in a highly regulated world. The shift from electronic medical record documentation of the care has put tremendous strains on hospice clinical staff. Until the complete shift occurs, the staff may be more focused on the documentation of the care than on the care itself.

Electronic medical records are required under the Affordable Care Act. The average age of many nurses in hospices is approximately 48, and some are not confident computer users. Hospices must train clinical staff on basic computing skills, which takes time away from patient care.

We now see hospice organizations struggling to manage within these parameters that the government has set, reset, and reinterpreted. They have had to retool how visits are made, how often they are made, who makes them, and how many patients each clinical staff member is responsible for.

To be successful today, hospice leaders must be strategic, pragmatic, and innovative. They must find creative ways to offer meaningful care to people at the end of their lives, within the parameters that the rates and regulations allow.

Dr. John Kenagy, who has written extensively on disruptive innovation, talks about how organizations must reinvent themselves as they go through their life cycle. As an example, he points out that the US steel industry was once the largest in the world, with great cities built around steel mills. As the ability to make steel improved, the steel mills began making finer and finer grades of steel and charging more and more for it. But they lost sight of the fact that rebar, the simple steel bars used in building concrete buildings, was made of the cheapest grade steel. In our quest to make the best and most expensive steel, we forgot about the massive rebar market, so Japan and other countries began manufacturing rebar and underselling US steel companies. In the course of 20 years, the major steel companies in the USA were undercut and, ultimately, went bankrupt.

It's a great analogy for health care today, and by extension, hospice. We have done the same things for 40 years. As we have coped with ever-increasing regulations and rules, new businesses and companies have been established which offer innovative ways of caring for people at home. New "rebar" programs beyond hospice include palliative care programs, transition programs, national physician groups visiting dying patients at home, advanced illness management, and more. The focus of health care has been treating illness. Now it is shifting to prevention of illness and empowering people to take care of themselves with support. While hospices are champions of that philosophy, we must prove to the other major health-care players that our expertise has always been in empowering patients and families. Today, it is still essential to ask the people using our service what is important to them. Some people may just want a basic "rebar" hospice experience, others may want a full complement of hospice services earlier in their illness.

Hospices must focus on their core business, which right now is the Medicare hospice benefit, while also putting time and energy into innovative programs. That might mean programs such as palliative care, PACE (Program of All-Inclusive Care for the Elderly), transition programs, or senior care at home. Create programs that have not yet been thought of. Hospice leaders must be asking, "What do patients and families need now? What do our partners in health care and social care need? What do the Alzheimer's patients and caregivers need?"

This last question will become increasingly important, as Alzheimer's will increase into epidemic proportions in the future. Not only do those afflicted by it need care, but their caregivers also need care. Ask yourself what you are doing now to prepare to serve those patients and families. What are hospitals going to look like in the next 10 years, and how can hospices help our partners serve patients in a more humane way?

We can no longer just sit back and think, "We're the community-based hospice and we don't have to play with anyone else." We must know what our competition is doing. We must know what our partners are doing. The new leaders moving forward must have, once again, that spirit of "anything's possible" while they maintain the status quo of where we are now, because we are on a very rocky boat. We are not sure exactly where the shore is, but we have to trust and believe it will appear.

LEADERSHIP AND THE NEXT GENERATION

Where will our next generation of leaders come from? Very often, the original hospice leaders came from social work and nursing and were more clinically focused. Then, in the 1990s, financial success became very important, so we began to see more and more people with business backgrounds and MBAs become hospice leaders. The new hospice leader must have a foot in each camp; in the clinical and the financial arenas. If we only focus on the business side of hospice, we will lose the tenderness and humanity of the clinical side. If you only have the clinical side, you might not survive financially to provide that care. You must balance the finances with service. A great leader is someone who honors and understands both points of view and the new world order.

That may be someone who comes from an innovative entrepreneurial background and who has had a personal experience with caring for a loved one. It may be the nurse with great clinical experience who also has an MBA and now brings a beautiful balance of both. Education is so much more accessible now. Anyone who wants to be in a leadership role in hospice will need an advanced degree, whether it is health-care administration, public policy, public administration, public health, or business. Understanding a balance sheet and a profit and loss statement is as important as understanding the parameters of how to dose morphine and make sure symptoms are managed. The bottom line is that we're going to have to do more with less.

I remember listening to an interview with Robert Rodriguez, the director of the movie *Spy Kids* who, on a very small budget, had created a huge box office success. The director said, "When you have less money, you have to be more creative. Sometimes more money does not always give you the best product."

Simon Sinek, author of the book *Start with Why*, wrote that companies that deeply understand why they are in business are much more effective and last longer than those that just want to produce a product. He used the Wright brothers as an example. The Wright brothers were not well funded, nor did they have college degrees; they owned a bicycle shop. But they had a deep belief that if they could make their ship fly, it would change the world, and that dream of flight drove them. Meanwhile, Samuel Pierpont Langley, a contemporary of the Wright brothers, was also trying to be the first to fly. The Smithsonian Institution had funded him, and the *New York Times* followed his exploits. He had money to spare and lots of people on his side. But his *why* was to become famous by being the first to master flight. Of course, we know the end of that story.

Sometimes, it takes being faced with fewer dollars to push us into being our most creative; we find a way because we must. We are at a point in hospice care and in health care in general where the innovators will be the ones who will come up with the new ideas, the new "rebar."

The coming generation of hospice patients will want something different from what their parents wanted. The "greatest generation" was more stoic in their approach to life and death. The baby boomers' needs and expectations are very different; they want to know, for instance, how they can continue to have intimate relationships with others, how to be medicated and not be in pain, preferably with organic drugs, and they are more open to alternative ways of care beyond straight Western medicine. Boomers will demand treatments such as acupuncture and healing touch and aromatherapy. Baby boomer caregivers caring for their parents are more informed and demanding. Adult daughters are typically making the decisions for both their children and their parents today. How can we best help them? We must be more customer service oriented now because the caregivers have already done their Internet research and will want to know why you are not giving her dad the massage therapy because the hospice down the street says they will provide it.

Going forward, we must be much more flexible, much more customer focused, and much more humble. In the past, not many people understood good end-of-life care, and we were seen as angels, but that has changed as this generation's expectations have raised the bar. We in hospice care must make sure we are changing along with, and indeed ahead of, our customers to be successful. We must, as Jim Collins said in his groundbreaking book, *Built to Last*, "Preserve the core and stimulate progress."

Chapter Three

"Companies should not have a singular view of profitability. There needs to be a balance between commerce and social responsibility... The companies that are authentic about it will wind up as the companies that make more money."

—HOWARD SCHULTZ

"Starbucks is not an advertiser; people think we are a great marketing company, but in fact we spend very little money on marketing and more money on training our people than advertising."

—HOWARD SCHULTZ

FOR-PROFIT VERSUS NOT-FOR-PROFIT MODELS

At its inception, hospice care wasn't a business model; it was a not-for-profit service model. Hospice Care Incorporated, later renamed Vitas, was the first for-profit hospice model in the country. In the 1990s, more and more for-profit hospice companies were created. As merger and acquisition activity increased, national hospice corporations were created and they began to be publically traded on the stock market.

The not-for-profit hospices stopped growing in number in 1998, and the for-profit hospice companies began to proliferate. In 2012, according to DMS, 32 percent of hospice Medicare providers were not-for-profits, and 63 percent were for-profits. While there are still many not-for-profit programs around the country, *consolidation* is clearly the watchword of the future. What hospice is experiencing now is very similar to what home health agencies experienced in the last century. This shift has made an impact on the type and quality of care provided. Through the 1980s and much of the 1990s, the not-for-profit hospices were their community's providers of choice. They were the ones who met their community's needs, because their mission was to provide care to dying people and their loved ones regardless of their ability to pay. Then, as the for-profit hospices began to flourish, many of the not-for-profits just said, "Oh, we will survive because we are the good guys and they are the bad guys." Many programs did not make any effort to change the way they did business, the way they accessed patients, or the care they provided. They just kept doing the same things they had always done.

Meanwhile, the for-profit companies approached referral groups, asking them to "give us a try; we can provide faster, better service, and we will meet your needs." Suddenly, referral patterns began to shift, and the not-for-profits' census started to decline. In many cities across the USA, large not-for-profit hospices had the market share until a number of competitive for-profit companies opened. These for-profit hospices approached physicians directly, telling them they would make physicians' lives easier and help them to take care of their patients in a more efficient way. Many not-for-profit program censuses went down while for-profit censuses increased. The attentive hospices reevaluated their own service models with a critical eye and ramped up their marketing and efficiencies to meet the challenge.

There are many communities across the country where multiple hospices are struggling against the stiff competition while all of them spend a great deal of money on promoting their programs. The larger national companies enjoy economies of scale by having back-office work done centrally, reducing overhead on the local levels. Most not-for-profit hospices have had to decide if they were going to compete in a new and more aggressive way and those that did have remained strong. The emergence of for-profit hospices has changed the entire movement, and uncertainty persists about who will survive the next few years. This phenom-enon happened to hospitals many years ago when benevolent groups opened hospitals for those in need. Government dollars began to flow into the operations of those facilities and then the free market took hold. Competitive for-profit hospitals brought more stringent business practices and forced the not-for-profit hospitals to either become competitive or go out of business.

THE IMPACT OF REGULATION

End-of-life-care costs are far greater in hospitals rather than in hospice care. These expenditures are being audited by various gov-ernmental agencies in search of fraud and abuse.

For instance, when hospice first began, we dealt mostly with cancer patients because treatment options were limited, and phy-sicians could predict with some certainty that a person with a particular type of cancer might have months rather than years to live. Today, thanks to medical progress, cancer, in many cases, is a chronic rather than a terminal disease. At one time, typically, 70 percent of hospice patients had cancer and 30 percent had non-cancer diagnoses. Now it is very nearly the opposite. Increasingly, hospices are serving people with end-stage heart or lung diseases, and/or who suffer from some form of dementia.

Recently, the CMS ruled that hospices could no longer admit those with a primary diagnosis of "debility or failure to thrive." As many people age, they suffer from multiple illnesses such as heart disease, diabetes, dementia and/or chronic obstructive pulmonary disease (COPD). Combinations like this are common among the very elderly; determining a primary diagnosis may not be clear-cut "terminal" diagnosis. As CMS continues to define hospice in medical terms, hospices must be vigilant in remembering hospice should be focused on human care. We are responsible for people's life experience until death, not simply their medical experience at the end of life. Hospices should be offering "patient-centered care" not "payment-centered care."

The not-for-profits hospices put financial gains back into their communities via increased services, while the for-profits put their gains into the shareholders' returns. I have observed both good for-profit hospices and bad not-for-profit hospices. Tax status doesn't make you good or bad. When poor care is provided to ensure large margins, it is unconscionable regardless of tax status. Hospices who invest back into their communities in meaning-ful ways are positively impacting people who are dying and their loved ones. The bottom line should always be high-quality care.

The infusion of for-profit hospices into the hospice movement has forced all hospices to focus more on sound business practices, and become more efficient in order to survive. However, the intense competition in many communities has jeopardized care. Choice is healthy, but for instance having 140 hospices to choose from in Atlanta results in confusion for dying patients and families. With that many hospices, qualified staff are difficult to find, competition is intense, and quality of care is often sacrificed.

DANGER AND OPPORTUNITY

The combination of danger and opportunity defines the Chinese character for the word *crisis*, and we are certainly at that point now in terms of the current crisis in health care.

Recently, I heard the president of the American Medical Association, Dr. Ardis Dee Hoven, speak. She noted a trend taking place over the last five years in which physicians in private practice are selling those practices to health-care systems and going to work for the system.

She also suggested the family practice physicians and the internists are gaining importance and influence in the system. In the past decade or two, it was all about the specialists. If you have been tasked with taking elderly family members to their multiple doctor visits, you understand. A recent study suggested that people in their 80s and older see up to six different physicians for care.

The new trend toward having a single doctor is taking us back to where we started in medicine, with the idea of the family physician. Dr. Hoven felt strongly that the baby boomers were going to demand this kind of care as they aged, which, ultimately, would offer more cohesive care. Hopefully all of this uncertainty and turmoil will lead to something that will be better than what it is replacing. It will take five to 10 years to evolve, and we are right at the beginning of the reform.

Hospices will need to partner with their fellow community players because in health care, the model is shifting to the patient as the number-one focus, with the system applying its services to that one patient. That means the successful hospices must learn to collaborate with the other community health-care organizations like: home care agencies, Alzheimer's associations, outpatient clinics, physician groups, the hospitals, the skilled nursing facilities, and the insurance companies to work together to provide the best care for patients and families. No longer can hospices believe: "We don't need to collaborate, we are just going to do our own thing." If you stick to that outmoded way of doing business, you will go out of business.

Many hospices are affiliating with or starting their own Programs of All-inclusive Care for the Elderly, better known as PACE programs. These are nursing home diversion programs aimed at elderly people who need supportive services such as adult day care, meals, or respite care. Samira Beckwith, CEO of Hope Healthcare Services in Fort Myers, Florida, has championed this collaboration between hospices and PACE across the USA. Dentistry, podiatry, speech therapy, and more, are part of PACE's all-inclusive care model for the elderly.

There are also hospices that own assisted living facilities, such as the Hospice of Marion County in Ocala, Florida. Some hospices have their own pharmacies, home health care agencies, physician practices, private duty programs, and palliative care clinics and programs. The ACA has made collaboration crucial for all health-care players. Hospitals are going to need fewer beds and hospices will need to have more beds. The more strong relationships a hospice has with key community health-care and social-care providers, the more likely the hospice will be seen as a vital part of the community rather than merely an agency that deals with the last few days of someone's life. One of the best examples of this community collaboration is HopeWest (formerly known as Hospice and Palliative Care of Western Colorado) in Grand Junction, Colorado. Since starting the program in 1993, Christy Whitney, CEO, has collaborated closely with the key health-care agencies (Rocky Mountain HMO, area hospitals, skilled nursing facilities, and public health agencies) to ensure every dying patient and their loved ones receive care regardless of setting.

Health-care reform will result in more hospice mergers and acquisitions, in both for-profit and not-for-profit hospices. Some not-for-profit programs are aligning their back-office services with trusted partners—billing, records, HR, legal services, and more—to save money and attempt to retain their identity while working with other not for-profits to combine or consolidate duplicative services. One program might have a quality or compliance department that's particularly outstanding, and another might have a finance/billing department that's top notch, while another might have a HR department that's first rate. Merging those services will make everyone stronger and cut expenses. I believe the willingness to explore these kinds of partnerships is going to be a measure of how many hospices will be able to thrive.

Palliative care programs are increasingly in the mainstream, with physicians trained and board certified in hospice and palliative care. Hospices should consider either partnering with hospitals and/or offering stand alone palliative care programs. At the moment, neither Medicare nor private insurances pay for full spectrum palliative care but rather pay for palliative medical consultation and intervention. The palliative care holistic approach to physical, emotional, and spiritual care can be provided to people who have years, rather than months, to live. Lastly, we must continue to thoughtfully support patients and their families to make decisions regarding medical interventions at the end of life. It is difficult for anyone emotionally involved to wrestle with the issues of what treatments are appropriate when an illness can only be stalled, not stopped. Sometimes the side effects of treatment are far worse than the benefits; it is not always a better life if you are miserable until the end. Helping people to understand the pros and cons of treatments with as much grace as possible will continue to be a significant part of our work in the future.

"If you want to build a ship, don't drum up people to collect wood and don't assign them tasks and work, but rather teach them to long for the endless immensity of the sea."

—ANTOINE DE SAINTE-EXUPERY

IT STARTS WITH STAFFING

The most vital aspect of any organization is its staff, and they are even more important in a service-oriented field like hospice. Your only product is the service your staff delivers. You have to make sure you are identifying the right people to do the work, to represent the kind of hospice you want to have. You must train and support staff, not only upon hire but also continually. And you must hold them accountable.

Hospice is a 24-hours-a-day, seven-days-a-week operation. People don't die Monday through Friday, nine to five, so you must make sure the people you hire are service oriented and have a real commitment to others. Having the right behavior is key. If you hire for personality, you can train for the job. Working in a hospice is unique because the patients we care for are dying. You must hire people, from the bookkeeper to the nurse's aide to the social worker or physician, who are comfortable with death and dying, because they are faced with it every single day. When you work with the dying, it forces you to think about your own mortality, your own family and loved ones death. You want staff who are emotionally stable and mature.

When I was hiring hospice staff, I used to look for people with a belief in something greater than themselves. I am not referring to religion, but to a faith in something bigger than themselves, faith in goodness, faith in humankind, faith in the rightness of the universe. When you are faced with death daily, it forces you to wonder what life is all about, what this mystery of life is and how you can make sense of it. People who are comfortable with who they are and are continuing to seek meaning in life make the best hospice workers. Why is this so important? Because, as Gretchen Brown, my friend and retired CEO of Hospice of the Bluegrass, says, "We only get one chance. We have one chance with each patient. If we mess it up, then it can impact peoples' lives in negative ways that we will never know. If we make it a positive experience, it can also have an impact on peoples' lives in profound ways."

Hospice care is a relationship business. That is why the first thing we have to do when we see patients and their family is to establish a relationship of trust. Most patients and families have not been exposed to death and may not know what to expect. We are the experts, the ones who can share with our patients, their families, and the community our wisdom about what is normal, what choices people have in their own lives, and how to live life to the very fullest.

You want to hire people who are curious, independent, confident and flexible, and who are able to think on their feet. We expect staff to go into people's homes alone and manage whatever situation is presented. In a hospital you can push a button and, instantly, many people will be there to respond to an emergency. But when you are alone in the home of someone who is very ill and dying, you must be the expert. You must project calm self-confidence and flexibility. That confidence comes with proper training. You must have a network of hospice staff your patients and their caregivers can call on when challenging situations occur. There must be a support system of hospice workers with expertise, not only for the patients/family to call on, but also for the staff as well.

We have cared for people living in less than ideal settings: homeless shelters, boats, campers without any utilities, or in cardboard boxes. You must hire staff members who understand that when they encounter a home that is substandard, it is still the patient's home and the hospice staff must not judge. If the home does not have heat or air conditioning, we must help them if they wish. If they do not have enough food, we connect them to community services to provide nourishment.

I have heard nurses who have visited a patient at home say, "That house is so dirty, we should discharge that patient because it is not safe for me to go in and sit down." That is not the type of staff person you want to have working for your hospice. You must ensure you can provide safe care, but we are on the patients' turf and we must adjust to their domain.

THE HIRING PROCESS

It's important to have clear and specific procedures in place for hiring staff, and that begins with the initial interview. There should be a set of questions that are automatically asked for each candidate. Hospice staff must recognize their own prejudices when working with dying people and families of different backgrounds. Hospice staff must leave their problems and prejudices at the patients' door, and if they cannot, they are not right for hospice.

There are many hiring tools available. I like the Predictive Index (PI), which is a talent management system that identifies someone's motivation and drive. PI looks at four key aspects of a person's personality: dominance, extraversion, patience, and formality. One of the PI's tools, the Job PRO which identifies the behavioral requirements of a job and then compares a person's personal PI profile to the job profile to evaluate fit. There are many, many tools available. Find one that fits and use it consistently. Incorporating analytics into your hiring process gives you a better chance of making an appropriate hire based on scientifically grounded data.

No hire should be made without a series of interviews. If you're hiring someone to work with a team, several of those team members should have a group interview with that candidate. Remember, the interviewers should never do all the talking. They should ask their questions quickly and succinctly and allow the candidates to answer them at length. If the candidate is not speaking at least 60 percent of the time, your interview process must be revamped. Probing questions should be asked, and the candidate needs to have the opportunity to give thoughtful responses. Questions to ask prospective staff should include the following:

- Have you had any personal experiences with death? Have you lost a loved one?

- What has been the biggest challenge in your life? How did you handle that?

- Have you ever worked with a team before? When did it work well, and when did it not?

- What are your personal values?

- How would you answer if someone were to say to you, "Am I dying?"

- If the prospective hire is a nurse, how will she/he handle a doctor who says, "I'm not going to give that patient morphine, it will make him addicted."

- What is the greatest accomplishment you have had? What is the greatest failure? How have you handled both?

- What do you like to do for fun and do you have balance in your life?

Once you hire someone, they must receive an in-depth onboarding process. That should include a review of the mission and the culture of your organization, and the expectations of the job, both functionally and behaviorally. So often, all we do is spend time on the practical aspects of the job: How do you administer the medicine? How do you document the medical records? How do you complete the forms? While those things are important, the most crucial aspect is how we expect you to behave as a representative of our organization, and a big piece of that is getting along with your teammates.

That means being kind and respectful. It means dressing appropriately. It means going into someone's home as a guest, not as the boss. It means asking people permission to call them by their first name, not just going in and saying, "Hi, Jimmy" instead of "Hello Mr. Jones." It means showing up on time and caring about your coworkers. New staff members must be clear on all that's expected of them, and that we will hold them accountable for these behaviors and expectations.

You should have a checklist of expectations, trainings, and systems that you have in place. Supervisors must make ride-along visits with all members of their team. Hospices are not made up of multidisciplinary groups; hospices are an interdisciplinary group, and that is a key difference. The interdisciplinary team depends on one another, values one another, and on any given day, any member can step up to be the leader of the team. It may be that the home health aide has more up-to-date information on a patient than the doctor or the nurse has; you may find that the social worker deals more with existential pain and management of the pain of loss than the nurse does with the physical pain. The chaplain can do a life review with people who are afraid of dying and think they are going to Hell, which can impact everything else in their life. There are no single heroes in hospice; if you cannot work with team members as equals, you cannot work in hospice.

It is also critical that you are able to leave your own troubles at the door. You might have just had a terrible loss or a fight with your loved one, but you have to be mature enough to say, "I'm leaving that at the door. When I go into this patient's home I will be present for this patient. I will be the one my patient can lean on, learn from, and be encouraged by."

A woman I know who is a hospice CEO told me about her experience in caring for her father who was dying. He was clearly terminal and was referred to hospice care. He was in the hospital and wanted to go home, but the hospice nurse said he had to stay at the hospital, because he was "too sick to be moved." The hospice CEO daughter said, "We want to take Dad home." The hospice nurse said, "No, no, he's much too weak. He can't go home. He has to stay here in the hospital and we will take care of him here." The next day, a different hospice nurse came in and said, "Oh, we are going to have to transfer your dad to the hospice house because he can't stay in the hospital any longer."

The daughter said, "Wait a minute, yesterday they told me he was too ill to be moved from the hospital. Today his condition is the same. We don't want to go to the hospice house; Dad wants to go home."

"No, no, he can't go home. He should go to the hospice house because we have everything there that we need to take care of him."

The daughter said, "No, this is not about you and what you need. This is about us. If he's well enough to be moved in an ambulance to a hospice house, he's well enough to be moved home." The nurse was flustered, but my friend had made up her mind, so hospice helped her achieve her father's goal of getting home.

He lived for two days in the comfort of his own home. She said, "My father was so happy lying in bed, looking out his front window, watching the birds on the feeder. He died a very pleasant, supportive death. But I shouldn't have had to fight to get my father home." And she's right; the response should have been, "How can we help you make that happen?" You must make sure that care in all settings represents the kind of care you want your hospice to provide.

THE IMPORTANCE OF ACCOUNTABILITY

One of the things I find in many compassionate organizations is that they are so compassionate that management sometimes has a hard time holding staff accountable for doing their jobs. Granted, hospice is a difficult and often emotionally charged job. It can also be the single most rewarding thing you ever do in your life: making a difference in the life of people who are dying. Helping to relieve pain and empowering people to stay in charge of their lives before they die are basic tenets of hospice care. Staff must also know how to take care of themselves. They must keep patient relationships in proper balance. We are not their families; we are their professional support system. We love them, and we care about them, but we cannot allow people to depend too much on us. We are in this line of work because we like to help others, and that is all the more reason why we need to be cautious about setting appropriate boundaries.

When patients die, staff may suffer too. Some patients allow staff to know them in a profound, intimate way. When a staff member has had three or four deaths in a week, it has an effect on them. Supporting one another is vital to maintaining emotional stamina. We must treat each other as we treat the patients and families we care for: with great respect, understanding, and kindness.

As a leader, you should be sure you have support available for staff. Encourage your staff in the ways they like to be encouraged, whether that's a hand written thank-you note, a verbal thank-you, or something said at a staff meeting. Likewise, when someone is not performing, it is imperative that you give that person appropriate feedback. If staff members consistently fail despite the fact that you have trained them, you have given them support, and you have given them feedback, then they may not be right for the job.

If that is the case, don't try to solve the problem by just moving people around in your organization. If, for instance, a staff member is not effective on the home care team, they are then transferred to another department where they may or may not be successful. They might be moved to yet another department after that. If they are consistently unsuccessful, it is time to move them out of the organization altogether. It may be the best thing for the staff member as well. It is important to the health of your organization that you are sure you have metrics in place to evaluate staff. Do not wait for an annual evaluation. Poor performing staff members should be receiving ongoing feedback regularly. If staff members do something inappropriate, their manager must give them appropriate feedback immediately. Feedback must include an overview of the infraction, options of doing it differently, expectation of how to do it in the future, and consequences of the action.

Staff must know the expectations of the job. In this new hospice world, there are fewer dollars, and the accountabilities are much greater. You must say for example, "I expect you to manage each of your assigned patients at a level you would be proud to offer to your loved ones." If they cannot achieve your organizational standards, then it is the manager's responsibility to determine the performance blockages to ensure the staff member is successful. Look at the top performers, see what their systems are, and help the lower performers understand how they can achieve the metrics that you are expecting, which means providing extraordinary care, documenting properly, and being part of a team. Having those metrics set up when you hire someone means there are no surprises; be clear about your expectations and if they cannot be met, be swift to make a change.

Hospice is not just about sitting at a bedside holding someone's hand. You are the expert. Whether you're the expert at billing or the expert at filing or the expert at bathing or the expert at identifying the medications that need to be adjusted, you must see yourself as the hospice expert, be held accountable for that, and hold your team members accountable to that level of expertise.

The best way to differentiate your organization from your competition is through the staff members level of expertise and the quality of the care they provide. Make sure your staff are highly trained, with the finest character. Some hospices require their clinical staff to have advanced degrees and the physicians and nursing staff to have hospice and palliative care certifications. Those are the kinds of measures that people will be looking for when they are trying to judge your relative quality. Consumers should be asking, "What kind of training does the staff have? What kind of education and background do they have? And what kind of people are they? What kind of expert care can we expect? How often will we be visited by each staff member?"

In hospices and in health care, the nursing shortage is tangible and it is going to continue as we move forward. Sometimes it is tempting to hire someone just because you have a gap you need to fill. It is always better to wait and hire the right person. Pull staff from other areas to cover until that opening can be filled rather than just settling for the not-quite-right hire.

Hospices should be the employer of choice in a community, and that begins with making sure that you treat your employees well, that you pay them as well as you can, and that your hospice is a great place to work. If you cannot be the highest-paying employer, then do the things that other employers cannot do. Talk about the importance of the work that's being carried out. Be supportive and encouraging of staff. Allow flexible schedules if you can. Increasingly, workers of this "sandwich generation" have to care for elder parents, ailing family members, and/or children, so flexibility is important, and schedules that accommodate their needs is a strong draw.

Accessing younger staff while they are still in school can give your organization an advantage, whether that means going to high schools talking to kids on career days or speaking to nursing or social work schools, be sure that when young people are making career decisions, they think of hospice. Make your hospice a site for student internships and be a continuous learning organization; give your staff education reimbursement to return to school for bachelor's or master's degrees. Work with schools to train home health aides to become licensed practical nurses, and then help LPNs to become RNs. If you invest in people early on, they will invest in the organization. Making sure that education and learning are core values of your hospice is a great way for you to stand out in the sea of hospices in your community.

Customer satisfaction must be a continuous focus. We must be kind. We must be responsive. We must be respectful. We must do what we say we are going to do, when we say we'll do it, every time. Your customers are, in many settings, not just patients and family members. When a doctor's office or a hospital calls and says, "We have a patient we'd like you to see now," be there as soon as possible, not the next day. We must be responsive to referral sources and ask what we can do to support them. Help patients achieve their last wishes, which may be to get out to the dock and go fishing one last time or to see a family wedding. Rather than saying, "Oh no, you shouldn't go out. It isn't safe," we need to do our best to make their wish happen. It is about the patients' wants and needs, not about ours.

Make sure that you treat your employees like the smart people that they are. They have ideas, so get them involved in projects. When they have complaints or problems, discuss solutions with them and/or ask them to come up with solutions. Organizations are like microcosms of families. Everyone has a role and if you can discover where people fit best, it will be a smooth-running operation with happy employees and happy customers.

I do believe that hospice work is "destination" work. It is not a place on the way to something else, not a résumé-building stop in which you think, "I'm going to work here a couple years and then go on to a hospital job." If the work is right for you, you stay; it becomes the fabric of your own life. For me, working with hospice has been one of the greatest gifts of my life. I have experienced a number of deaths in my family, and without the hospice work experience, I would not have been able to get through those losses with as much grace and understanding as I did.

The bottom line is, when you're hiring people, hire for personality and dedication and commitment to serve, and then train them to be the very best hospice workers they can be. An organization is only as good as good as its weakest employee. If you have employees who are not kind, who do not show up when they are supposed to, or who give the wrong information, that story will be told 20 times by the family, and your reputation will suffer accordingly. It is incumbent upon managers to ask themselves, "Is this someone I would want at my bedside if I were dying?" And if the answer is no, then don't put that person out in patients' homes to do untold harm.

Chapter Five

*"If your actions inspire others to dream more, learn
more, do more and become more, you are a leader."*

—JOHN QUINCY ADAMS

RECRUITING MANAGEMENT AT THE EXECUTIVE LEVEL

A significant part of my practice is executive recruiting. It is crucial for any organization, not just hospices, to assemble the right leadership team. The CEO/ED sets the tone within the organization and the executive team carries out the strategic plan. It is crucial that the board of directors hires the right CEO/ED, and then allows that person to create a high-functioning executive team.

What do we look for while recruiting leaders? It is not simply what is on the résumé. While experience, education, and background are important, the more critical qualities are their character, values, personality, and passion for the work. Organizations reflect the personality of its leader. If that leader is a gregarious, risk-taking, adventurous person, she/he will drive the organization in that direction. Conversely, if she/he is a cautious, careful individual who is not comfortable with risks, the organization will reflect that style as well.

The first step in hiring a CEO/ED is an assessment by the members of the board of directors of their vision for the organization's future. Do they want to grow? Do they want to maintain the status quo? Do they want to expand into new service areas or geography? Evaluate the current status of the organization to determine if it is stable and growing or shrinking. Is it stagnant or in financial trouble? What is the culture of the organization? Is change embraced or challenged? Those questions and more are the keys to identifying the next successful leader. Once the board members decide on the vision for the future, they can look for a leader who will take them there.

Sometimes, when replacing a CEO/ED with a long tenure— more than 20 years—it is not uncommon that the next leader becomes the change agent who typically may not stay long. It is the person who follows that one who is often the next successful, long-term leader. Boards should be aware of that phenomenon, and temper their expectations of what is likely to happen in the first year or two after the exit of a longtime CEO/ED.

An internal candidate who has been groomed for the job is ideal. Identifying future leaders within the organization and fostering people who want to move up should be ongoing. If you hire a CEO/ED from within, there should be a seamless transition when the change is made

If you do not have that potential leader waiting in the wings, external candidates must be brought in. In the past, people with clinical backgrounds like masters prepared nursing or counseling or social work with a business background were preferred. Nowadays, a CEO/ED must understand not only the increasing emphasis on the business of the organization, but also the clinical operations. It does not mean candidates must have an MBA, but it does mean they must understand financials, profit and loss statements, and gross returns on investment. This is the kind of expertise that hospice leaders of the past did not always have. However, entrepreneurial experience is important for the hospice leader of the future, as much as it was at the beginning of the hospice movement.

Very often, boards of directors make the mistake of having the current CEO/ED be actively involved in the search for the next leader. Leaders who have been in the position a long time may want to ensure that their policies, visions, and culture remain intact. The likelihood is that they will recommend a candidate who can be the kind of leader they are. Consequently, there may not be fresh points of view brought into the organization.

The board of directors should take full responsibility for the CEO/ED search by forming a search committee and hiring a recruiter with industry experience. Often the committee is made up of executive committee members and/or former board chairs or founders. Hiring a recruiting firm allows the board to stay focused on the mission while the professional recruiter identifies candidates.

When conducting a CEO/ED search, based on the board's vision and direction, look for candidates with experience in hospice, and/or those in leadership positions in similar organizations, candidates with passion, excitement, and vision for the future of our industry. At a minimum, candidates must understand what it takes to ensure a positive bottom line, provide enlightened customer service, inspire a culture of caring and accountability, and have an unwavering focus on quality care, while being innovative and realistic.

Should the board hire a CEO/ED with only a financial background and/or business expertise, they must ensure the leadership team is balanced with those having clinical expertise to ensure clinical excellence.

Look for candidates with a connection to the region or area. Just because someone has a great résumé does not guarantee a perfect fit. Your candidate must be thrilled about the community in which he/she will live or they are likely to have a difficult adjustment. Some type of personal connection to the region is essential.

Next generation hospice CEO/EDs must be innovative and comfortable with change. They must be risk tolerant, customer focused, and engaging. They must work together with other health care and social care agencies and be nimble and quick to adapt. Sometimes, organizations are so stuck in tradition that they are like an ocean liner that takes a long time to make even a small course change. Today hospices must be flexible enough to adjust rapidly to market changes while maintaining stability and accountability in the changing health-care waters.

The CEO/ED must be a big picture visionary while understanding the demands of day-to-day operations. However, in smaller programs, those with fewer than 75 people on staff, it is inevitable that the leader is closer to the day-to-day functions. But remember, if you want your program to grow, your CEO/ED must have the bigger picture in view, always asking how the organization fits into the larger community, how best to serve the citizens of the service area, and identifying customers' and referral sources' needs.

A search should result in a variety of candidates to choose from and objective, science-based tools should be used to assess the candidates. As I mentioned earlier, my preference is for the Predictive Index, but there are other tools to assess the personality of candidates. Be aware of candidates who know how to interview brilliantly but may not have the capacity beyond an interview.

When I was the executive director of Hospice of North Central Florida (now Haven Hospice), we searched for a new chief financial officer. We interviewed a number of candidates and settled on a final candidate who seemed terrific. She had education and experience that matched our needs, having worked with a large home health agency as well as a company that had managed fund development. And she was delightful. During the interview, she answered every question I asked in exactly the way I hoped she would. At the end of the interview I said to her, "You're just too good to be true." She smiled and shrugged her shoulders. She interviewed with my senior team. They all loved her. She interviewed with our corporate partner CFO, who quizzed her about her financial expertise. He was very impressed with her. She interviewed with one of the executive vice presidents of the hospital with which we were affiliated. He thought she was perfect.

We made her the offer, pending a successful background check, drug screening, and fingerprint check required for that level position. When I told the candidate about the background check, she said, "I'm recently divorced, and I changed my name, and my purse was stolen, so I don't have my IDs," which meant we could not copy her driver's license for our files. Then, the background check came back showing a conflict between her married name and her maiden name.

The compliance person said, "We need to do the next round of background checks, which is going to cost a little more money, just to make sure we've got everything in line." We kept calling the candidate to say, "Can you give us your Social Security number?" to which the candidate replied, "Oh, I don't have it because my purse was stolen."

She had given me three references. I was only able to reach two. One said, "All we are going to say is she would be eligible for rehire." Hmm. The next reference was a man for whom she had worked at a private company. He said she was the best employee he'd ever had and terrific in every way.

The second layer of background checks revealed that the first name she had given us had a tag on it for an arrest. She had embezzled $600,000 from a previous employer. She was out on probation. And that glowing reference? It turned out that the man to whom I'd spoken on the phone was her father! He had kept the telephone in his pocket waiting for my call. The home health agency staff member who had said the candidate was eligible for rehire didn't want to say anything negative because the agency staff members were afraid she would sue their agency. Had we not taken the time and done a little more digging, we would have ended up with a CFO who was a convicted felon out on probation.

Don't be fooled. If you interview someone who seems too good to be true, keep pulling the strings to make sure that it doesn't unravel into a tragic tale. Do your due diligence and then do some more. Scan the Internet for your prospective hires, look at social media sites, and follow up on anything that looks questionable. I worked with a client who had hired a vice president of quality. The person had been onboard one week when someone on the staff Googled her name and turned up her mug shot for a drunk driving arrest. The CEO spoke with her, and she told him a story about having had a fight with her boyfriend that involved the police, but she had not been arrested. Remember, not everything on the Internet is true, so verify the good, bad, and the ugly. It turns out that person did not survive that organization because she was not a fit with their culture.

The culture of an organization is crucially important to understand when hiring a new leader. Whether a CEO/ED or a vice president or a director, the "fit" has to be right. It does not matter if you are a Harvard graduate with 20 years of experience in hospice care. If you are not a good fit in terms of culture and personality, it is not going to work. If you are in a conservative part of the country where people are more focused on home and family, your next CEO/ED should reflect those values. Maturity matters and is a quality you should look for in leadership. It is not maturity in age, but rather, in life wisdom. I have worked with 35 year olds whose life experiences had deepened them and given them wisdom beyond their years. I have also met some surprisingly immature executives twice that age.

In your interviews at this level, you must talk to people about death because that is the business they will be in. Ask questions such as: Have you experienced the loss of a loved one? How do you deal with stress? How do you deal with staff members who are facing their own challenges? Are you someone who holds everyone's toes to the line without flexibility, or can you hold people accountable and still be understanding when life situations occur? Workers of the new generation are different from their parents. They want quality of life, they want flexible schedules, and they want time off to be with their friends and families. Leaders must understand the needs and concerns of the multiple generations of workers from the baby boomers, generation X and Y, and the millennia's.

The new CEO/ED must be comfortable with the broad spectrum of responsibilities that comes with the complex business of hospice. Delivery of high quality professional care in a variety of settings, financial stability, fundraising, successful partnering with multiple organizations, local, state, and federal governmental regulations and oversight, policy reform, engaging volunteers at all levels, hiring and inspiring all levels of staff who will do this emotionally charged work well, day in and day out in a changing health care market, all with death as the overarching connector, are just some of the responsibilities of the hospice leader.

As with staff, it is important that your next leader view the job as "destination work," not as résumé-building work. Look for candidates who want to fully invest themselves in their work, who are not only interested in the organization but also invested in the community. There are examples of people who have been in banking or run other non-health-care businesses who have stepped into the CEO/ED jobs at hospices and been successful. But, generally, those people will have a long learning curve. Look for candidates who are passionate about this exquisite work, and who will balance the mission with the margin.

CREATING A SUCCESSFUL SEARCH COMMITTEE

The board of directors' search committee must be balanced with people who deeply believe in, and understand the mission of the organization. They must also understand the dynamic needs of the community and they must have the time to devote to this crucial task.

In terms of numbers, four to six committee members is ideal. The search committee must be united in the kind of person that they want to hire. Do they want someone with hospice experience or not? Do they want someone with clinical experience, or does that matter? Do they want a local person? Do they want someone with a national background or experience, so that they can bring their organization to a national level of prominence? Do they need someone to stabilize an organization that is out of control, or do they need a change agent who is able to make the difficult decisions? They should be united in what they and the entire board are looking for.

I have worked with boards whose search committees are made up of their executive committees, which can be very efficient. The committee should be empowered to make decisions quickly. Search committee members will need to select the recruiting firm, identify the profile of the ideal candidate, interview candidates, select the best person, create the offer, and present the candidate to the entire board. The search committee members should have an understanding of the health-care arena and the mission of the hospice. You want members who are committed to the future success of the organization, who understand its history and the current challenges. People with a human resources background are great too because they understand the fluidity of a search process. Having the chairman of the board, or a vice-chairman, on a search committee is helpful because they can make executive decisions quickly.

The selected search firm should spend time with the search committee and the executive team and should get to know the organization and the community. They must gain a clear understanding of what sort of candidates will be successful and the key challenges of the organization. The search firm should examine the organization's financial status, the previous surveys from the state and federal agencies, and results of any national accrediting agency reports. As an executive recruiter, I also look at the organization's complaint logs and staff turnover, volunteer base, philanthropy experience, and quality scores because all of those things will play a part in determining the kind of person who will be successful. The more the search firm and search committee clearly understand those issues, the more likely it is they will achieve the best match.

Once the references are checked and the offer is made and accepted, the board chairman and executive committee must make sure that they have expectations and goals set for the new CEO/ED. If they have not, then the CEO/ED should develop them and make sure that the board chairman clarifies those goals and expectations. If the board just says, "We've hired you. You go do your work," and does not give any guidance, there could be significant gaps by the end of the first six months or year. There should be close communication with the chairman of the board and the new CEO/ED, and it's crucial that feedback flow in both directions.

When CEO/EDs are hired, sometimes bonuses are involved, often tied to various performance metrics. That might include stabilizing the organization, or growing the organization, or a positive bottom line or a turnaround, but the bonuses should be tied to some specific, measurable performance metrics. When looking at bonus structures/evaluation structures include growth and financial metrics, quality care, community and staff satisfaction as a part of the calculation. This might include what your quality scores look like at the end of the year, the number and types of complaints received and how they were handled, and what patients and families are saying about the organization.

Another key measure is the state of staff engagement. Very often, new CEO/EDs will ask a hospice consultant to conduct a baseline organizational assessment to determine strengths and gaps of the organization. An outside view can be very helpful to a new leader to gain insight into the challenges they face. Often, community involvement or fund development is also used as a metric in measuring the CEO/ED's performance.

Whatever your criteria, there must be a clear-cut, shared understanding on the part of the board and the CEO/ED of what is expected. In turn, the CEO/ED should lay out the same kinds of expectations for their executive team, so there are no surprises about how success will be measured. It does not fall on the shoulders of one single person. The CEO/ED sets the tone and hires the executive team, but ultimately, it takes everyone working together to achieve those common goals and reaffirm them regularly, not just within the executive team but throughout the organization. Make sure that everyone is moving in the same direction and accountabilities are strong.

A healthy level of trust between the CEO/ED and the chief financial officer (CFO) is extraordinarily important. That combination can make or break an organization. Trust must exist because if the CEO/ED wants to go off in new directions and start new programs, the CFO should be strong enough to say, "What is the return on the investment? How much is it going to cost? Maybe we should do it next year instead of this year." Likewise, the financial person has to trust that sometimes the CEO/ED might make decisions that do not, on paper, look like the best ones, but in the bigger picture are the right things to do.

SUCCESSION PLANNING

If you are the current CEO/ED and you know it's likely that you'll be leaving in three to five years, begin now to identify those people on your current team who might have the capacity to grow into replacing you. The best strategic visionary might already be working in your organization. If you don't have that candidate on board now, keep your eyes open for the leadership qualities you seek in the next person you interview for a position with your hospice. Then mentor them so they are ready to fill a more important role than the job for which you hired them.

I have a friend who was a director of clinical services at a small hospice. She knew she wanted to be a CEO and shared that ambition with her boss. She said, "It was a risk. I know. I'd been there about seven years, and I wasn't sure if she knew my long-term goals, so I told her, 'I want to be the CEO of this organization one day.'" The CEO was a little startled, but she said, "Okay. Then let's get on that path." Three years later, it happened.

Always refresh your cadre of potential leadership candidates, even if it is one or two people every couple of years. Bringing in people with new ideas is key to keeping an organization vibrant, and it is a great way to ensure smooth leadership transitions.

Chapter Six

"People will forget what you said, people will forget what you did, but people will never forget how you made them feel."

—Maya Angelou

WORKING WITH VOLUNTEERS

One of the unique things about hospice care is that the federal Medicare hospice benefit requires volunteers to provide 5 percent of their hours in patient care. No other Medicare benefit requires volunteer involvement. The commitment to volunteers was brilliant because it engages communities in the act of caring for the dying.

One important measure of a quality hospice program is the number of active volunteers and their level of involvement. When I work with a hospice and conduct my consulting assessments, one of the first areas I ask about is: The volunteer department; How many volunteers do you have? What kinds of things do the volunteers do for hospice? How long have they been volunteering? As we move forward in this new world of hospice and health care reform, volunteers are going to have an even greater impact on the lives of people who are facing serious illness and death. Volunteers want to have a meaningful way to contribute and hospice is a remarkable place to achieve that.

What kind of person is likely to volunteer at a hospice? Most often, volunteers will be people who have had a positive hospice experience through having cared for a dying loved one, and they want to give back in a meaningful way. Once their own acute grief has subsided, they can be very effective volunteers with patients and families who are going through similar situations.

Don't overlook younger people who want to discover meaningful ways to serve others. Hospices offer a great opportunity for younger people to utilize their energy and enthusiasm in a mutually beneficial way. Some will want to work with patients; others may want to work on a specific project. From doing office clerical work to involvement in philanthropy, community presentations, kids' camps, choirs, or committee work, volunteers are vital to hospices.

New volunteers may find it challenging to go out to patients' homes alone. Encourage them to initially go with a staff member, and then offer them support often. Patient care volunteers must be independent and confident and have no personal agenda but to serve. They should know their own limits and understand when to call the staff for support.

Very often, the simple act of sitting with a patient so the caregiver can go to the bank or hairdresser or grocery shop is a tremendous gift. Sometimes, the patient and caregiver just need a friendly visitor, someone who knows what they are going through. A social worker might offer counseling, and the chaplain is there for life review or prayer, but the volunteer can just listen like a friend with no agenda or goal except support and love. When friends/family visit patients, they themselves can be distraught and not able to give the support that the patient or families need. It is the hospice volunteer who can provide that neighborly strength and caring.

Many hospices have volunteers called eleventh-hour or vigil volunteers. When someone enters the final stages of death, the family may be exhausted and/or distressed. Eleventh-hour volunteers are on call to sit with those patients until the patients' death. It is a sacred act to be witness to another human being's journey from life to death.

Another great volunteer opportunity is in the Tuck In program, in which trained volunteers call patients to say, "Hello, I am a hospice volunteer. I want to make sure everything's going well for you and see if you need anything before the weekend. Do you have enough medications? Are you having any problems we can tell the nurses or doctors about?" These friendly callers remind the patients/families of the caring aspect of the hospice and they reduce the number of calls over the weekends. By being proactive instead of reactive, the patients/families needs are met before they have to ask.

Hospices all around the country are using volunteers to do many creative things such as video life reviews, making new flower arrangements from funeral flowers, being clowns at kids' programs, and leading bereavement groups. Teenage volunteers who have either experienced the death of a loved one or who just want to give back can be a great support to kids with a parent who is dying. A more active volunteer department works closely with schools and clubs, senior groups, faith-based groups, and more, to offer opportunities for people to give back. As I toured a hospice house one day, the smell of freshly baked chocolate chip cookies drew me to the kitchen where I found a group of girls from the local high school. They told me that once a week, they came to bake cookies for the families and patients in the hospice.

Volunteers can be the greeters who give tours of the facility, or they can help in the kitchen. Some hospices engage with local garden clubs that provide flowers or create lovely settings outside patients' windows. At our hospice in Gainesville, Florida, volunteers from the local koi club maintained our koi pond and local artists and musicians provided performances and art exhibits. Using volunteers at your hospice is a great way to engage the community to become involved.

Engaging with faith communities is a natural link for a hospice. Offer hospice volunteer training to those who are involved in specific faith communities so they can support their own members who are facing death or grieving.

TRAINING AND ACCOUNTABILITY

Recruiting and training volunteers is the first step in creating a vibrant volunteer corp. Then, supporting them, holding them accountable, and recognizing their contributions should be done in thoughtful and prescribed ways. Decide what types of volunteers you want and focus your recruiting on those groups. Some hospices advertise upcoming volunteer training in local papers. Some put fliers in retirement communities that have active adults who are looking to contribute.

Volunteer training must give people a clear understanding of what is expected of them. The curriculum should include an overview of the organization and its mission, vision, and goals and an understanding of the stages of dying. It should also include listening and communication skills practice, and a review of volunteer job descriptions so volunteers understand what is expected of them and whom they go to for help. Be sure that you include confidentiality requirements and training on how to work together as a team. Some hospices do training in three hours; some hospices' training lasts three weeks. The average number of hours spent on volunteer training is 8 to 12. The National Hospice and Palliative Care Organization offers comprehensive volunteer training manuals that are excellent. More and more hospice programs are offering segments of training online via videos or webinars, so volunteers can access them from home. Face-to-face training time should always be included when volunteers are going to be serving patients in their home.

Volunteers should be held as accountable as your staff members, and that means giving them their assignments and expecting them to follow through. If they cannot make a visit or will be late for some reason, they must call in, just as paid staff members do. Make them a part of the team because they represent your organization. There should be an annual review of each volunteer just as there is of the staff. Determine whether they feel supported by the team, whether communication is strong, and whether they are performing up to the expected standard and/or if they want to try another activity within the organization.

Make sure you do not have volunteers who are on some type of crusade or have a personal agenda to "fix" people. The focus should always be on what the patients need, not what the volunteer needs; it should always be about the patient and family. When interviewing potential volunteers, be alert to each one's personality. Not everyone is suited to work with dying patients. There are many other kinds of useful work that volunteers can do.

Just as with staff, it is vital to recognize volunteers. April is National Volunteer Month, and luncheons or dinners or awards presentations make people feel valued. More importantly, throughout the year, saying "Thank you" is essential. Staff members are busy doing their work and may assume someone else will be taking care of the volunteer appreciation. But volunteers give their time freely and a heart-felt thank-you, both written and verbal, from the staff can be a treasure.

Volunteers can be essential in the fundraising department. Many not-for-profit hospices have events ranging from extravagant galas to bake sales at the local farmers' market to fashion shows. These events cannot happen without a vibrant volunteer group.

There are also professional volunteers who may offer massage, aromatherapy, Reiki, music, and art therapy. Music is such a powerful part of the human psyche. If you cannot afford a music therapist, look for local choral groups that can work with your hospice. Look for people in your community who have unique skills, unique gifts, who might want to offer their gifts to dying patients and their families.

Another important role volunteers can play is in pet therapy. Many hospices work with the owners of therapy animals. These people bring their pets to the hospice or to patients' homes, allowing the patients to interact with a variety of pets from dogs and cats to llamas or horses. It is an amazing thing to watch. If patients have been dog lovers in the past, sometimes even patients who appear to be unresponsive will react to a dog or cat when it is put in their lap. It is a very healing experience for the family members as well.

Many programs use volunteers as adjuncts to their social workers, counselors, or chaplains in supporting the bereaved. Our hospice had a group of volunteers who were specially trained to identify stress triggers for at-risk family members who were bereaved. They made supportive calls to family members, following the death of the patient. Professionals most often lead bereavement groups, but if a hospice wants to have a more social approach to bereavement, such as getting people together to have coffee and support one another in a casual way, volunteer leaders can be used. We also worked with local artists who would hang changing exhibits of art in our offices and our hospice house. University students may need to accrue volunteer hours, so use them in creative ways to support patients and staff. Your local library may sponsor a book group for your hospice or send volunteers to read to patients. We had a massage therapist who did shoulder massages just for the staff because she knew how hard it was to do hospice work. We had hairdressers who volunteered to go out to someone's home or come into our hospice house and do patients' hair.

A great thing that Halifax Hospice and HopeWest Hospice offers are memory bears.

With the family's permission, volunteers use pieces of clothing belonging to the loved one who died to craft a memory bear that they give to the family. Many hospices have thrift stores or resale shops staffed almost entirely by volunteers. Families can donate the total contents of households to the resale shop, which raises funds to support hospice.

Does your organization properly value your volunteers? When I see hospices that have a volunteer coordinator who is four levels away from the CEO/ED on the organizational chart, that suggests the CEO/ED may not value volunteers. A volunteer director on the leadership team is very valuable and will ensure volunteers are valued in deep and meaningful ways.

As hospices receive less and less money from Medicare, and as more baby boomers enter active retirement, matching volunteers with patients needs will be vital. A happy, fulfilled volunteer is a great hospice ambassador to the community.

Chapter Seven

"People don't buy what you do, they buy who you are."

—BRUCE TURKEL

HOW TO COMPETE

I f your care is superb, delivered consistently and unfailingly goes above and beyond what is expected, you will be the top provider in your community. Period.

When hospice began, there was no competition because there was no money involved. We were doing something noble that not many other providers wanted to do.

Over the last 10 years, an explosion of hospice growth has taken place. In many communities, hospice competition is fierce. Until the for-profit movement came on the scene, the word *sales* in the hospice community was never used. But in today's competitive climate, all hospices must be well versed in what *sales* means to them. The Merriam Webster dictionary defines *sale* as: the exchange of goods or services for money. Are you in the business of sales? Exchanging goods and services for money? Or are you in the business of *marketing* your services, which means the activities that are involved in making people aware of a company's products? Or both?

Knowing what your points of differentiation and excellence are is exceedingly important. Every hospice is required to offer basic things under the Medicare hospice benefit. What makes you stand apart from your competition? It is not simply your tax status of for-profit or not-for-profit. The key differentiators are the quality of care that you provide, the responsiveness you show to patients and families, physicians, and referral sources, and commitment to your community.

Your marketing/sales staff should be separate from your care provision staff. Often there is tension between those two groups because the marketing/sales force's job performance may be measured by the number of admissions. The people who do the care giving want admissions to be scheduled regularly and without surprises. Both groups should report directly up to the CEO/ED via vice presidents and/or directors who monitor growth and quality performance.

In a competitive market where there are multiple hospices, being timely and doing it right the first time is crucial for success. Determine how long it takes from the referral—the initial phone call informing you of a prospective patient—to when your staff first visits that patient face to face. It should be a matter of hours, not days. Sometimes, when families call, they are not sure if they really want to admit their loved one to a hospice. Understandably, that is a very difficult call to make and we must be sensitive to their needs. We also must believe the kind of care that we provide will make a difference in the quality of life of the dying person and their family's lives as well. The more swiftly we can engage with that patient and family and help them have that lifeline of support, the more at ease they will feel.

Know what makes you different; know what makes your hospice excellent. Everyone in your organization should be able to answer the question, "Why would I choose you? Why would we choose this hospice instead of that one?" Every staff member should have the salient facts at their fingertips and might say, "All our physicians are board certified in hospice and palliative medicine," or, "Our nursing staff are all hospice and palliative care certified," or, "We have the greatest patient-to-staff ratios compared to other hospices." Whatever your differentiators are, be clear on what they are and why they make you a better choice for that referral source. Then ensure every staff member knows the differentiators and lives them.

Be easy to work with. If a hospice staff member puts up more blocks than avenues of welcome, referral sources will label you as difficult to work with and go to the next hospice on the list. Be supportive of, and responsive to, your stakeholders. The stakeholders can be physicians, their staff, hospital discharge planners, skilled nursing facilities, assisted living facilities, and others. These are the places where patients live and receive care. If we can be responsive and easy to work with, if we can say, "Yes, we can," more often than "No, we can't," we will build the kinds of relationships we need to grow.

I worked with a small not-for-profit program in a rural part of the United States. It had been the only provider in the area for years and had done everything possible to support its community. Within two years, there were five national competitors all vying for the same patients. The competitors hired local people who had relationships with the largest oncology physician practice. The hometown hospice with 25 years experience in the community began losing its market share and census. Why? Because the other hospices' staffs were saying, "How can we help you? Give us a try, let us show you we are responsive." That's how competition works. You cannot stand on your past history of longevity or simply being a not-for-profit. You must offer great care and great customer service. Do what it takes to do it right the first time, on time, every time.

If someone makes you angry or a referral source is difficult to work with, you cannot say, "I'm not going to admit any of those patients from that nursing home because they are so hard to work with, and their care is not that good." That's exactly who you should work with because those hospice-eligible patients in that nursing home need you more than they would in one that has fabulous care and friendly staff. We must be able to adjust to the needs of our patients and families and referral sources. We must be kind and respectful. Again, even if a physician is demanding or challenging, we must adjust because, at the end of the day, it is always about the care we know we can provide for dying patients and their loved ones.

In looking at ways to be customer service oriented, take a tip from the hospitality industry. Danny Meyer, the New York City restaurateur, whose restaurants are as famed for their incredible service as they are for their amazing food, published a book titled *Setting the Table: The Transforming Power of Hospitality in Business.* Sometimes I think we believe hospice is only about health care, but really, we are about hospitality and humanity, and gracious-ness of service. It doesn't mean that the customer is always right, but it does mean that the customer always has to be listened to and acknowledged. Staff must be flexible, and they have to be kind and thoughtful as well as smart.

Make sure you have the right people in the referral/admissions positions because that is the front door to your hospice. If you have crabby, grumpy folks answering the phone, callers' first impressions will negatively impact every subsequent interaction they have with you.

In order to be competitive, know what it is your community really wants. Often, hospices offer programs they think are important but which may not really meet the needs of their community. Great organizations get to know, intimately, what their customers want. That means spending time with patients and families, not just sending out a survey that can collect some bits of information. It may be transportation that patients need instead of massage therapy. They may need someone to support the children in their family and the primary caregiver. Consider having administrative staff members make a dedicated effort to pay visits to patients' homes at least twice a year to ask the patients and families, "What is it that you all really need that you are not getting now?" You will discover valuable information.

Do the same with the largest referring sources. Spend some time in physician offices sitting at the desk with the nurse who answers the incoming calls. What kinds of issues are they faced with? What kinds of issues are the physicians faced with? How can you help support them in the job that they are trying to do?

You must also look at how your hospice manages customer complaints. If you have complaints without proper follow-up your competitors, if they are responsive, will have the edge on you. Having a proactive way to deal with service failures or customer complaints is vitally important to your success.

You must know what your market share is. There are data mining groups that can tell you exactly what percentage of dying patients are using your services and what percentage are using your competitors' services. You need to know where you stand in the market. If it is not as good as you expected, take a hard look at your program or start asking your referral sources, "How can we better help you serve your patients?" And really listen to what they tell you.

Sometimes, it is useful to have a third party consultant ask those tough questions for you because referral sources may not want to complain to someone they know, particularly in smaller communities where people know one another well. Have a consultant do a market assessment to identify how easy or difficult it is for physicians and referral sources to work with your program. Listen to that feedback and make adjustments. You must know the data in order to move forward.

Also, look at who is hiring the marketing/sales staff, and to whom they report. Those reporting lines are crucial. I worked with a hospice that had a very smart, aggressive marketing vice president. He had a business background and understood the metrics of marketing and sales. He hired marketing staff who measured their own success by how many appropriate new referrals or admissions they could sign on. Those marketers were dispatched to teams and reported to team managers, who were responsible for the day-to-day operations of the clinical care.

The marketing staff would go out to visit doctors' offices and say, "We'd like to help you with your hospice-eligible patients because we believe we offer extraordinary care." Then they'd come back and report to the team manager, who would say, "Oh, no. We don't speak to the doctors that way. We wait and let them send referrals to us because we don't want to be pushy."

Unsurprisingly, those marketers began to quit within the first year. That was because the person who had hired them was not the person to whom they were reporting. The team managers were not convinced that the more aggressive marketing model was the right thing for their teams. It is vitally important to make sure everyone in leadership is on the same page. Staff must know what the rules are and make sure that they are responsive to the needs of the patients and referral sources. They have to be able to balance marketing and provision of care.

Transparency is becoming increasingly important. Daily, post the census to all employees. All staff members should share responsibility for the success and growth of their organization. It is important that everyone from the nursing aide to the physicians are able to articulate why they believe their program is the best. For instance, when you are standing next to someone in the grocery line who says, "Oh, I see your nametag. Tell me about your hospice," your staff must be able to respond. It is not just the marketing team's responsibility to market the hospice. It is the responsibility of every single person in the organization to be able to say in three minutes or less why their organization is the very best and why they work there.

The Affordable Care Act is changing health care, and we will see new partnerships between former competitors. Hospices need to make sure they are at the table with Accountable Care Organizations (ACOs), which are paid by Medicare to improve individuals' care, improve the health of populations, and decrease health-care costs.

Often it will be a large health insurer, a health system, or a large physician practice that will set up ACOs, and hospices must be equal participants. No other organization can provide better care at the end of life in people's homes than a hospice. There are certainly home care agencies that know how to keep people at home and manage episodes of illness, but hospices understand from a health-care, as well as a human-care point of view what people need to be safely and compassionately cared for in their homes. Claim your expertise and create innovative partnerships in our new landscape of health care.

It's also important that your organization have an active, engaged presence on social media. That means actively participating on Facebook, Twitter, Pinterest, Google+, LinkedIn, AboutMe, and others to engage the community. Having an informative, interactive and up-to-date website is an absolute requirement. Social media resources are no longer optional; they are essential ways in which people find you and connect. As members of the younger generation take on responsibility for the care of their elders, they are not going to look in a telephone book. They are looking online, comparing quality scores, and reading your reviews.

A lot of organizations make "service promises," in which the marketing department lists "the 10 things that we will do to make sure we provide the service that you deserve." Those are great if every person in the organization lives them. Service promises should be consistent from the clinical side as well as the marketing side because there is nothing more damaging than breaking a promise.

You have discovered what your patients want; now, discover what matters emotionally to your referral sources. For the physicians, knowing that the hospice promises to visit their patients, 24 hours a day, seven days a week matters. Your hospice must support physicians when they deliver that difficult diagnosis of, "I'm sorry.

There are no more treatments for your condition." If your staff can offer training to physicians on how to share difficult news and then offer support to those patients and their families who have just received that news, a tremendous service to both doctors and patients will be done.

Make sure your patients are prepared for an environmental or climatic crisis—for example, a pending hurricane or a major snowstorm can be a tremendous stressor for patients and families. Your organization's preparations and follow-through is a differentiator from your competitors. Having your disaster plan in place for emergencies will make your program stand out because people will know your patients will be cared for and kept safe.

Above all, you must understand and live within the hospice laws and regulations. Knowing what you can and cannot safely provide within the confines of the laws is not negotiable. Directing patients to places that offer services that you don't offer is part of great customer service. For instance, when a patient's caretaker says, "We want you to be here 24 hours a day because I work all the time and mom is lonely," don't cut off the conversation by saying, "No, that's not what we do." Instead, say, "Medicare does not allow for that under the hospice benefit. Let me give you the names of three private duty agencies that can provide that kind of support, and we can work together with them and use our volunteers to help you with a plan."

When you're assessing your customer service, think about how you would like your loved ones—your mother, your father, your spouse, your child—to be treated if they were facing a terminal illness. Be consistently kind, professional, respectful, dignified, and positive; patients and their families need that as much as they need medications. We must be the strong, wise, supportive encouragers to help them along their journey. If your care is superb, delivered consistently and unfailingly, and goes above and beyond what is expected, you will be the top provider in your community. That is the most effective way to be competitive. Period.

Just as we anticipate and plan for birth and birthing, a new movement is forming around "deathing." How we choose to live the last days of our lives is very important to all of us. We want to have choices. We want to be in charge of what is happening to us. If hospices can be responsive to those issues and encourage conversations about living with intention until you die, we will be at the leading edge once again.

The programs that provide exquisite core hospice care and develop new innovative ways to support seriously ill patients and their families and stakeholders will be the organizations that succeed. Now is not a time to just adopt a business-as-usual attitude. Today, more than ever, it takes boldness to lead. You must have staff that think creatively and are not afraid to speak up and say, "Maybe we should do this differently." It is as important to make sure that innovation is alive and well in your organization as it is to keep the core business going. Embracing both is the key to the next phase of hospice success.

Chapter Eight

*"Far better to dare mighty things, to win glorious triumphs, even
though checkered by failure, than to take rank with those poor
spirits who neither enjoy much nor suffer much, because they
live in the gray twilight that knows not victory, nor defeat."*

—THEODORE ROOSEVELT

THE ABUNDANT FUTURE

Philanthropic futurist Leanne Kaiser Carlson and I work together on hospice strategic planning retreats. Her central message is about changing the mindset of boards of directors and leaders from one that is resigned to shortage, lack, and being a victim of governmental reductions, to a mindset focused on an abundant future filled with new opportunities and innovative ways for people to engage and contribute. In this chapter, the focus will be on the not-for-profit hospice organizations and foundations and what they can do to enhance their development activities.

People want to give to successful organizations. If they see that a hospice is struggling and shrinking in size, significant donors are likely to turn away. Not-for-profit hospice leaders must ensure the operation is efficient and financially sound. You must be good stewards of the dollars received from all sources. The Hospice Medicare Benefit allows for basic hospice core operation; everything else beyond the core service should be funded from your philanthropic dollars. Some communities expect their not-for-profit hospices to offer such extraordinary care that they contribute donated dollars to achieve that high level of care. If your donor base believes in what you do, keep it up. Being good stewards of all the assets that come in is a sacred trust.

Successful development and stewardship starts with the CEO/ED's commitment to making sure that the hospice is run efficiently, that the hospice is engaged in the community, and that the hospice is seen as a resource in the community for people who are facing serious illness.

REACHING YOUR DONORS

If the hospice is invested in its community, philanthropic gifts are more easily realized. There is a multitude of giving opportunities for donors, from memorial donations to in-kind donations of goods or services, grants, or event support. These are passive ways hospices receive donations and have a great opportunity to increase those kinds of gifts with little effort.

Focusing on planned giving is a tremendous advantage to long-term survival. Fostering relationships with people who may not give today, but who have estates that they may want to leave to a worthy cause tomorrow, is a great long-range strategy. While it is not going to help in the now, when those significant dollar gifts do come in, it will ensure stability in terms of how the hospice can impact the community.

While fundraising events are time consuming and may not always offer large returns, they can raise awareness and establish alignment with your organization. Make sure that your events reach a variety of potential givers, not just the big-ticket donors but also the smaller ones who would like to see themselves as stakeholders as well.

Direct mail is another common strategy. Generally, this takes the form of a heartfelt letter from a patient, family member, board member, or a volunteer who talks about their personal experience with the hospice, why they gave, and why they would like you to give. While direct mail usually includes a self-addressed envelope in which to return a check, the most frequent method of donation is now through online donations.

Again, hospices must be sophisticated in social media and must be out there telling their stories in media-friendly ways. Put a link on your website to videos of patients or families saying, "Thank you so much. Your donation allowed me to have..." Then, the patient describes whatever the donation funded, for instance: "Pet therapy has made such a difference in my life. I love my volunteer and the therapy dog that comes to visit me. It's really helped me get through some tough times." The video doesn't have to have a big price tag. This kind of 30-second or one-minute video can be made on someone's smart phone. It lets donors meet the real people who are being impacted by their donations.

However you do it, make sure it is easy to donate to your organization. Just as you make it easy to be admitted to your hospice program, it should be uncomplicated to make a donation.

If you want to have vibrant fund development activity in your organization, you have to hire people with experience who understand fund development. It is best to assign an experienced fund development professional who understands the psychology of giving to take charge of the philanthropy department. Decide if you want to have a separate foundation in your organization or if you want to simply have a specific department that's dedicated to that task. There are pros and cons to both.

A foundation can have its own private 501(c)(3) tax-exempt number. Its sole purpose is to raise money to support your hospice and palliative care organization, and it will have a separate board of directors. Those board members should be donors and people who know others who could become donors. It is a different group of people from those who are on the operations board of directors. You should have representation from your operations board on the foundation board and vice versa, but the foundation board members should understand that their sole purpose is to raise money and make friends for the hospice operation. Those monies stay in a separate account and your hospice accesses them through policies and procedures that are established through the foundation. The foundation should have its own executive director who reports to the CEO of the hospice. Fostering a strong link between the hospice operation board and the hospice CEO/ED is crucial both to the foundation and the hospice organization. Some organizations find creating a foundation too cumbersome, but others find it a safe haven to have their donated dollars separated from their operations dollars. That's a decision each board of directors and CEO/ED must make.

If you do not have a foundation but have a fundraising department, the person in charge must have a very senior title; for instance, executive vice president of fund development, or chief development officer. That way, when they are fostering relationships with potential donors, the donors know they are speaking to someone who has the power to make decisions. The chief development officer should work hand in hand with the CEO/ED.

Everyone in a hospice or palliative care organization can and should play a part in fund development. If you wear your name tag in public, people may say, "Oh, my friend was taken care of by your hospice. Thank you." Your reply could be, "I'm happy you had a good experience; we operate through the generosity of others. If you'd like to make a donation, just go online." Very often, clinical staff believe it is intimidating or inappropriate to ask for a donation because they want to keep the money separate from their care. Today we must make a connection between the care that's being provided and the healing component of the generosity of giving. Just as we feel good when we do something that makes people feel better, donors can gain that same sense of accomplishment if they have the opportunity to give to the organization that made a difference in their loved one's life. Making sure that we create these emotional connections with donors *during* the hospice experience, not after, is key.

Provide training to physicians, nurses—all clinical staff—on how to tell the story of hospice and the power of generosity and its power to heal. Make it a part of their jobs. Then, when a family says, "I wish there were something I could do to thank you," your staff will feel comfortable saying, "A lot of other people have felt that way. In fact, our hospice got started from the generosity of a few donors in our community. Because of them, we are now serving hundreds [or thousands] of people a year." Tell stories about the how donated dollars have made an impact on patients you serve.

Stories are powerful. Making that connection with people is what makes all the difference in whether they give a little or give a lot. Realize too that there are donors out there who may not seem capable of giving large amounts but actually can and will. Sometimes, the least expected person can give the very most because of an emotional connection.

How does your organization thank people? Does every donor receive a signed letter from the CEO/ED? How long does it take to get a letter of thanks? Is the donor's name spelled correctly? There's nothing more frustrating for a donor, whether that person has donated $5 or $500,000, to receive a letter that has the wrong address, the wrong name, misspellings, or some other error. Letters must be heartfelt so that donors know that the investment they have made to this organization is genuinely appreciated. Be sure you're doing something special for larger donors. Make the thank-you experience exceptional so donors will say, "I gave to the hospice and you will not believe what I got in return. I got a personal telephone call from the CEO and a hand-written note from the children at the children's camp," or "I got a photograph of a hospice family saying thank you." Make the thank-you that you give to big donors so extraordinarily meaningful that they'll want to give again and again.

Engage artists in your community to create poems or songs or art pieces and present them to donors. Have a choral group of three or four go to the donor's home and sing a song to express their thanks. Be creative about finding innovative ways to say, "Thank you," and be sincere.

Always follow up with donors. After they have given, ask their opinion of the experience. Annually ask your donors, "Is there anything else we could be doing for you? What else would you like to know about our organization? How can we make sure we are showing our gratitude to you, as a donor?"

If you improve your donor retention by 10 percent, you will have a 100 percent increase in your donations. Look at your donors list to determine if they were passive donors as in a memorial, or an intentional donor via a direct ask. If you get to know your donors in a more in-depth way, you will generate more loyalty and create lifelong donors.

BUILDING A SUCCESSFUL CAPITAL CAMPAIGN

If you are planning a new building, establish a capital campaign committee, which is made up of people who only serve on the capital campaign and may not necessarily continue to serve as board members. Their sole purpose is to raise money for this one project. It could be an endowment, or a building project, or an innovative program. Select members for the committee who can either give money themselves or who have direct connections with people who have wealth. Then, make your case statement about why this particular project is important and have a timeline and a dollar goal for what you need to raise. Offer a variety of events and ways of giving to this particular campaign.

Celebrate when your benchmarks are reached and make sure that the community knows the progress you have made toward achieving your goal.

Fund development staff should be customer-focused professionals who understand it may take a long time to work with people before they make a donation. Helping donors understand what you do and getting them invested in your organization can pave the way to larger donations.

Your fund development department or foundation outcomes are only as good as the people you have on staff. Recruit staff experienced in fund development, whether from universities, faith-based communities, or service groups. Ask potential candidates how much money was raised annually by the organization they currently work for, ask about their direct contributions to accomplishing the financial goal, and ask how many staff they work with. Ask to see samples of the statements of intent and brochures they've created.

Hospice leaders must recognize that to survive, they must innovate. Some donors will want to invest in your innovations. For instance, develop new ways of caring for seriously ill people, not just hospice patients. Once or twice a year have an innovation day when your staff get together and discuss solutions for needs of patients and families, community members, and grievers. You will find donors who will want to invest in various kinds of innovation because, as the baby boomers approach the end of their own lives, they are going to be looking for new tech-forward, pioneering approaches to care.

It is also important to quantify the impact of the donation. For example, specifically tell prospective donors, "We provide services for everyone regardless of ability to pay. Your $100 donation will allow a patient to have a bed for a month, or three weeks of medication, or six home health aide visits." Make your message tangible so people understand that if they were to give $5,000, they could provide hospice care for a patient and his family for three months. Making that heart connection for the donor is critically important.

Create a card with a story that illustrates how donations impact the work of the hospice. When someone says to a hospice worker, "I wish there was some way I could repay you. The hospice has given so much to me," the hospice worker can pull out that card as an example of what hospice donations can do to help others.

People who are dying want to know that their legacy can live on, whether through a program, or a scholarship, or a brick with their name on it on the patio of the hospice house. Have a whole range of ways in which donors can be a part of the work. Establish a variety of creative gifting opportunities from landscaping your grounds to children's grief camps. Think outside the box, and remember you're giving people a way to put meaning into their lives. Give them an opportunity to experience gratitude—theirs and that of those they have helped.

It is not just about asking for a donation; it is about giving people the opportunity to be generous as well. Hospice is not just about physical care; it encompasses social care as well, caring for people's social well being, their emotional health, and their spiritual health. Once gratitude and appreciation are part of the foundation of your hospice, the organization can reinvest in ways that are unimaginable.

Do heroic things and give donors an opportunity to be heroic as well. Your donations will increase in many different ways. So often, not-for-profit hospices rely on being poor and asking for discounts and financial breaks. Their mantra seems to be "Poor me. Give to me." It serves you better to proclaim, "We want to do more for our community. We want you to work together with us to make a significant difference in our community." That's a more inspiring mission statement than "We're poor, help us."

Chapter Nine

"One thing I know: the only ones among you who will be really happy are those who will have sought and found how to serve."

—Albert Schweitzer

WORKING WITH A BOARD OF DIRECTORS

Having a solid working relationship with your board is key to having a successful organization. Particularly in the not-for-profit world, the board functions as the oversight of the organization and, in a sense, has ownership in the organization. Boards of directors can be extraordinarily dynamic, leading organizations into a brighter future. They can also be so cautious that the organization never grows. It is crucial to make sure that the right people are in the right seats and working together as a team.

What is the purpose of a board? Board members set the vision and the mission, and provide the strategic direction of the organization. It is the leadership and staff that put those visions, goals, and strategic initiatives into operation. The board's job is to ensure the mission is achieved, that there are proper resources to do the job including financial, personnel, and infrastructure, and to monitor the CEO/ED's performance. Board members serve as the overarching guides, holding leadership staff accountable for the success of the organization.

Ideally, boards should ask themselves four questions: the strategic question of "where should we be headed?"; the operational questions of "what is happening now?" and "how do we get from the now to the future?"; and the accountability question of "are we keeping the covenants that we've made with the community?".

Who is your ideal board member? Look for a balance of community leaders who will bring in the perspective of the community's needs, and who will share with the community what hospice and palliative care can do. Having key health-care leaders on your board is important; for example, a physician who is a significant referrer and/or hospital CEO who understands the health needs of the community. Also include business leaders and/or financial managers and leaders in the senior care community. If you're looking to have donors sourced by the board, someone who is in banking or who works with wills and estate planning is an obvious choice.

Everyone who comes to the board should be able to contribute dollars, even if it is only $50 at the annual golf tournament, or $100 a year. When a prospective donor asks, "Does your board support your organization financially?" if you cannot say, "One hundred percent of our board makes contributions to our organization," that prospective donor might not be willing to make a gift. When I was the executive director, we were engaged in building a new facility, and we applied for a major grant through a national funder. The person helping us complete the application said, "You know, we don't have 100 percent of our board as donors." I said,

"Oh, that's okay. That's not going to matter." We sent in the application and we were denied in part for that very reason.

Your board should be as diverse as the communities you serve, particularly if you have a wide-ranging service area. A balanced board doesn't have to be large. Between 12 and 15 members is a good number to be manageable. With a board of more than 20 members, it becomes difficult to keep board members involved and engaged and to achieve the cohesion that lets them work together effectively as a team.

Whose responsibility is it to find those people, and where do you find them? First you must have a great mission and a great organization to which people are eager to donate their time, energy, money, and support. A high-quality organization attracts high-quality board members. One of the board's jobs is to look for new board members and to vet them appropriately. Members cannot just say, "Oh, yeah, he's my buddy and we play golf together. It'd be nice to see him at the board meetings." I think it is important to have people who have experienced hospice and understand its value.

What groups do you want represented? That depends to some extent on your needs. I have seen boards made up of people who can provide an organization with specific kinds of support. Such members might include an attorney who can help with contracts, a banker who can explain where to invest, a CPA who can help with the financial oversight, and someone in marketing who can go out and speak for the hospice. That said, at some point you have to back away from asking board members to contribute their professional expertise and ask instead for referrals to people they would trust to provide expertise in their place. Otherwise, there could be a conflict of interest or ethical challenges. If a board member's CPA firm wants to be your auditor, they can participate in a bid process and be on a level playing field with others. Conflict of interest signature forms must be created and signed for all the board members every year.

The board should have oversight in terms of the quality and compliance of the organization and be well informed about the appropriate quality measures that apply. They should make sure a yearly, external financial audit is done, and a budget is completed. They should also be aware of what is happening in the community in terms of where the gaps in care are. They need to understand what the issues facing hospice are nationally so they have a big picture view in order to lead their organization into the future. It is the role of the CEO/ED to be the bridge between the board and the staff members who are doing the work and to see that the goals of the board are appropriately set and met.

Have clear policies for the board, and written job descriptions for the board members. Identify the duties of the executive committee members, the chairman, the vice chairman, and the treasurer. List what is expected of committee chairs, and what the roles of the individual board members are. There should be a board orientation manual that includes the mission, vision, and values of the organization so that every board member understands the organization's working parts. It is the responsibility of the executive committee (via the CEO/ED) to ensure new board members are appropriately trained and understand their roles.

New board member orientation must go deeper than spending an hour in the hospice office going over organizational charts and forms. Board members should be assigned to go out and visit patients with staff so they have an understanding of the sacred work with which they are entrusted. Seeing the impact of hospice at the bedside can be illuminating. It also means committing to supporting the organization and attending meetings, fundraising events, committee work, and generally, being an active participant. Board membership ought not simply devolve into a status symbol: "Oh, I am on the hospice board and that looks good on my résumé."

Boards should be involved in the big issues—Do we want to change our name? Do we want to start an adjacent business? Do we want to merge or acquire?—rather than the more routine matters such as policy updates, processes, or staff reassignments, which are the responsibility of the CEO/ED. I have seen boards waste an entire meeting talking about the wallpaper and carpet choices for a new hospice house when their focus should really have been on identifying a great person to contribute a significant gift to the new building.

You must be very aware of what kind of member you need when you're recruiting for your board. I have seen a situation in which a board chair brought in a friend, and then another friend, and then another friend, and eventually created a coup to oust the CEO. The board chair and her friends convinced the rest of the board that what they were doing was right. They fired the CEO and proceeded to appoint one of themselves to be the interim CEO, ultimately giving that person the full CEO title. Their appointee had an intense business background and began to run the not-for-profit community hospice like a manufacturing company, and several years of turmoil ensued. Finally, the other board members said, "This isn't working and we need someone with hospice experience to be the CEO." They ultimately got the hospice back on an even keel, but it took a great deal of focused attention and collaboration. Proper selection of board members is vital to the success of a hospice.

As in all things, balance is key. Sometimes boards can get caught up in focusing too narrowly on regulatory issues, or focusing too much only on quality. Then, all of a sudden, growth stops, or the financial status gets out of balance. Similarly, when you concentrate too intently on the bottom line, quality can suffer.

The most essential job of the board is choosing a CEO/ED. I am involved with a large number of boards in my work as an executive recruiter and consultant. Strong organizations have board members who understand the issues within the organization and recognize what is needed in the future leader.

Trust is crucial. I have seen CEO/EDs who make the board of directors somewhat superfluous. When a new board chairman takes office, and the trust between the CEO and board chairman is not present, the entire organization can suffer. Once a seed of mistrust is planted, it is very difficult to dig it up and start over. A board member once said, "Trust is like a tree; it can take 30 years to grow and just 15 minutes to cut down." It is the responsibility of CEO/EDs to make sure they know each board member personally and are in sync with the executive committee and vice versa. That relationship needs to be both transparent and harmonious. It is the role of the CEO/EDs to make sure they meet at least once a month with the board chair to discuss issues the CEO/ED is facing and needs a board decision on. CEO/EDs should not take for granted that their board will run itself.

The role of the chairman of the board is crucial. The chairman is the captain of the ship, and the CEO/ED is the pilot. The chairman must take his/her role seriously. Often it means putting in a lot of unpaid hours. One of the most difficult decisions comes when a board decides it doesn't have the right leadership for the organization and needs to make a change. That falls on the shoulders of the board chair and the executive committee to begin the change. There are times when closed sessions are required to discuss the CEO/ED's performance or a sensitive staff issue without management present. Afterward, the board chairman should inform the CEO/ED, "These are the issues we have discussed, and this is what we'd like to see resolved." The chairman should not overprotect the CEO/ED or the staff. If something isn't going right, or the CEO/ED is not performing, or there is a sense that there's discord between the staff and the CEO/ED, it is the board chairman's responsibility to look into the situation and decide if it is something minor or something that needs action.

The board chairman must understand visionary leadership. Do not elect a chairman of the board who does not understand what it takes to lead. We often see board members who are executives in their own businesses and who want to be involved in the hospice operations the way that they are in their own business, and that's not useful. I have heard board chairmen say, "I want to be here once a week and I want the staff to come to me and tell me what the issues are because I want to be involved in fixing them." That is not the role of the board chair or the board. The board sets the vision and mission and is involved with strategic oversight, not the day-to-day operations.

I have also seen situations in which board members who've been involved with the organization a long time have developed close personal relationships with staff members. Then if something goes awry, like the CEO/ED creates a new policy and the staff complain to their friends on the board, it can be harmful to the organization. Staff members who have issues with the CEO/ED must go through the proper channels in the organization, which is most often via human resources (HR). If something is illegal or immoral, and HR is not responsive, of course staff should go to the board chairman only, and the board should investigate, or have an outside consultant investigate the allegations. It is very important to make sure that there is not a direct path between the staff and the board in terms of complaints. Otherwise, the CEO/ED is marginalized and trust is broken and the organization will be at risk.

Sometimes, when a board is faced with a crisis, such as the firing of a CEO/ED, the board gets involved in the operational leadership of the organization. Then, when the new CEO/ED comes onboard, it is sometimes difficult for the board members to step back from being so involved. Maintain a proper balance by having the board govern and the CEO/ED lead.

It is vital that the board hears not only from the CEO/ED but from the executive team as well— from the senior leaders responsible for quality, finance, and for the clinical teams—so that there is a balance of information being shared with the board.

Richard Ingram sums it up well: "Boards and board members perform best when they exercise their responsibility, primarily, by asking good and timely questions, rather than by running programs or implementing their own policy." Board members should be asking the right questions. When something doesn't seem right, the executive committee must decide if it is an issue that needs further investigation and take action if necessary.

The board needs to evaluate itself as well. An annual board retreat is a great time to ask, "What did we accomplish last year, and what goals do we have for next year and the year after?" I think it is very useful to bring in an outside facilitator for that type of meeting, someone who can provide the information on national issues affecting hospices and how other hospices are innovating. If you don't know what is happening in the bigger world of hospice and palliative care, it is impossible to make informed decisions about the future of your organization.

As part of this regular self-evaluation, board membership should be reviewed. Questions such as "Do we have the right members?" and "Are we appropriately diverse?" should be asked. That issue in particular is one every board and organization must face, moving forward. Your board members must proportionately reflect the diversity of your community as your staff members do. Diversity of age, gender, ethnicity, thinking, and background are at issue. Younger members should be included who can bring important perspectives in terms of what their age group needs and wants from the organization, and how the organization can better serve them.

Make your board meetings meaningful. Many organizations are moving to meetings without agendas, for which the minutes, the finance report, and the operations report are sent out ahead of time and are approved at the beginning of the meeting. The bulk of the meeting is then spent on strategy. Are your meetings ones at which your board simply listens to reports and approves them and has no input in the organization's future? Or are you engaging board members who ask questions about what the community needs and how your hospice can provide it?

Make sure that your bylaws are updated regularly, that there are term limits, and that they are enforced. I facilitated a strategic planning retreat for a board that had no enforced term limits, and there were board members there who had been on the board for 20 years without a break. We began to review the mission statement, and one man raised his hand and said, "I don't know why we are doing this. That mission statement just sits in a drawer and nobody looks at it. It's a waste of my time and of everybody else's time." I was so taken aback that I didn't quite know what to say. He didn't really want to be there; he just liked the status of being on a hospice board. Fortunately, one of the newer members spoke up on the importance of having a meaningful mission statement. Be sure that your board has term limits, and if you have someone who is clearly no longer invested in the work of the board, then it is the job of the executive committee and the board chairman to usher him or her out.

Make sure that your committee meetings are scheduled for the entire year, that you have an agenda, and that you're prepared. Send out the board information at least one week in advance of the meetings. Many hospices have purchased iPads (usually at reduced prices) for board members to receive all the board documents, using a software application to manage the information. Having an efficient staff person running the operations of the board is very important; it may be the executive's assistant or a part-time senior assistant assigned to do board follow-up and committee work.

The CEO/ED should touch base with the board chairman in the days following a board meeting to go over the issues discussed and what the CEO/ED intends to do to follow up. The CEO/ED and the board chairman must be on the same page, and it is the CEO/ED's responsibility to see that that happens.

When a board is functioning well, it is a beautiful thing to witness. There are ebbs and flows in every organization just as there are in every part of life. Organizations that have a well-functioning board do not overreact when the census is low and the bank account is empty. They keep their balance. They also do not get lackadaisical when things are going smoothly.

Lastly, in building boards, hospices need to look at creating mutually beneficial partnerships. I have worked with several boards around the country that have structured board membership to have permanent seats on the board for representatives from the prominant health-care systems in the communities they serve. For instance, in Pittsburgh, the large not-for-profit hospice, Family Hospice & Palliative Care, has permanent board seats for the large health-care systems, the large senior center system, and the smaller hospital systems, thus allowing for investment in the hospice by the major players in the area. Moving forward, consider guaranteeing seats on your hospice board to leading partners in your community. These alliances and collaborations will be increasingly important moving forward in the new health-care arena.

Chapter Ten

*"Until one is committed there is hesitancy...the moment
one definitely commits oneself, providence moves in.
So, whatever you do, or dream you can do, begin it.
Boldness has genius, power, and magic in it."*

—GOETHE

TO BUILD OR NOT TO BUILD

I n spite of the regulatory scrutiny and possibility of rate reductions in hospice, I see a building boom in our future. The coming wave of baby boomers will mean that we need to be ready to provide the care they will demand as they face the end of their lives, and hospice facilities will be part of that equation.

The conversation about death has changed considerably since our movement started 40 years ago. Hospice has positively impacted health care, social care, and the way people look at dying. Hospices that are committed to serving their communities must ultimately decide on their commitment to freestanding facilities—hospice care centers—where people can live their last days in comfort, with staff and volunteers who are well trained in caring for people who are dying. These care centers are places where not only are the patient's needs met but the family's needs are as well. A hospice care center can provide tremendous relief for the patient and the family members, an oasis of calm in a chaotic world.

We built our first hospice care center in Gainesville, Florida, in the 1990s. When family members came for a tour to decide if they should bring their loved one there, they would initially walk through the front door, anxious, afraid, and uncertain. As we walked down the art-filled hallways and they took in the soft colors, the smiling staff, and the warm, comforting atmosphere, you could see them visibly exhale in relief and say, "Wow, I didn't even know a place like this existed." The stress of having to make that tough decision just melted away, replaced with confidence that their loved one would be in a place that was beautiful, and filled with people who understood what they were going through and would manage their care with respect for their wishes.

From a business point of view, care centers are very challenging to operate. There are some freestanding hospice facilities that have a positive bottom line, but it is not easy to accomplish. A break-even bottom line should be considered a success. Before beginning a building project, the first thing any hospice should do is a feasibility study to determine whether or not there is a need in the community, whether or not there is sufficient fundraising capacity in the community to support the building, and whether the hospice itself has the infrastructure to support it. An experienced consultant who understands not only the financial side of these operations but also the community side should complete the feasibility study. This study should include interviews with referral sources: physicians, discharge planners, and community leaders. There should be well-supported answers to a number of big questions including: Are there other big fundraising efforts competing for donor dollars right now? How much money was raised for the last community service that built a building (e.g., YMCA, or a faith community program)? What is the community capable of? Hospice leaders sometimes assume that a smaller community will not turn out to support them in sufficient numbers to make a building project feasible. However, the level of support you can find when it comes to hospice can be surprising.

A strong feasibility study must include a strong financial assessment: What are the costs? What are the hidden costs? What are the ongoing costs? I have seen situations in which a donor shows up with an enormous donation toward funding a building project, and the hospice eagerly commits to the project without doing the homework on its long-term sustainability. How many years will it take before the hospice can break even? How much money will have to be raised to ensure that the operations can draw upon that endowment for the center?

Each state has different regulatory laws in place for hospice, and the Medicare hospice benefit suggests, in general terms, what a hospice in-patient facility is required to have. But you must understand what the productivity standards should be and what kind of staffing models you want, whether that includes only RN and nursing assistants, or a blend of RN, LPN, and nursing assistants.

Your staffing models should drive the design of the building. I have seen larger, older hospice houses where that wasn't the case. I worked with a program that had 16 beds on one side of the building and three beds on the other side of the building, so the nurses were constantly running back and forth. Make sure you take your productivity standards into account, and use them as a guide for the architects when they begin a design.

An important question is where to locate your facility. One thought might be to locate it on a neutral campus, with an easily accessible spot in the community. If you want your hospice services to align with a particular health-care system, your building should be on or near that campus. Do you want to build in a growth area where new development seems likely in the future? Or do you want to remodel a place in a more depressed area of the community that you know could be turned around? Home and Hospice Care of Rhode Island in Providence was given an old, multistory nursing home from the 1940s that had fallen into serious disrepair, and they turned it into a work of art. It has helped to revitalize the neighborhood and has become a focal point in the community.

The demands of running a hospice care center are very different from those associated with a home-based hospice operation. You must continue to keep your eye on the ball after the house is built. Your beds will need to be kept full with the appropriate kinds of patients, and you will have to maintain the staff to care for them. It is a 24-hours-a-day, seven-days-a-week, 365-days-a-year operation. There is no down time. That creates a different kind of stress and operation from that of a home-based hospice service, where the offices close and an on-call night team takes over.

What is currently available in your community? Are there other places people can go to get good care at the end of life, or is there a gap? Be sure that you're filling a real need before you take the step. As they say in construction, measure twice and cut once.

You should also consider the case mix of patients you want in your facility. When we opened the hospice house of the Hospice of North Central Florida in Gainesville in 1995, it was primarily a residential facility. People could come and stay for weeks or even months and pay a room and board fee and receive hospice routine home care. What we quickly discovered was that the people who came there needed a lot more care than we had anticipated. We expected that there would be a fair amount of patients who might be able to walk to a dining room to eat, who could feed themselves, and who could be up and around. But because of changes in regulatory demands, hospitals began to discharge patients whose needs were complex. When those hospice patients could not be managed at home, they would want to come into the hospice facility. That meant we were caring for people who often could not get out of bed, who sometimes had to be fed, and who sometimes needed IVs, and in 1995 we were not staffed for that level of intensive hospice care. We had to retool ourselves as well as our staffing models to make sure we had a higher level of staffing to manage the patients' intense needs.

Today, much shorter stays are normal, with an average stay between four and nine days at a hospice care center for acute-symptom management for those near death.

Most hospice care centers have the majority of their beds dedicated to patients who fall under the Medicare-designated billing code of general in-patient level of care. General in-patient (GIP) care is short-term, crisis-intervention, symptom-management care of the dying. Changing medications, managing pain that is out of control or other difficult symptoms are approved at the hospice Medicare general in-patient level of care.

Community hospices should also consider at least a few of what we call "residential care" beds if possible. These beds will serve the needs of patients who are able to pay room and board and want to stay longer than the Medicare GIP level allows for but who don't have any other place to go or family caretakers available. Having a few residential beds in your mix is very important for a balance in the community. It is important to consider ahead of time the impact of those beds on your financial performance and to plan accordingly. For example, consider a 12-bed care center with two beds that are designated for residential care and 10 beds that are designated for general in-patient care. If those two residential beds are full, and you have empty beds on the GIP side, the temptation is to fill the bed with anyone in need, but remember that a residential patient will be paying a much lower rate than the GIP rate. If you fill the beds just to keep them occupied, your financial situation gets out of balance and begins to tip because you now have more patients who are paying less, and a staffing ratio scaled for the higher level of general in-patient care. Suddenly, you're losing money and putting the entire organization at risk. Even if it means keeping those GIP beds empty until you can fill them with appropriate patients, it must be done. If you were running a hospital with an ICU, you would not put someone recovering from a broken arm in the intensive care unit simply because there was an empty bed there. You have to make sure your case mix stays in line with your productivity standards to manage the costs.

If you decide to build a care center, make sure you have an architect who understands designing health care facilities, because there are strict regulatory construction rules for health care facilities. The architect's expertise in this area can make a big difference to your bottom line, now and in the future. For instance, having oxygen piped in through the walls, rather than using canisters, will save you money in the long run although it may be initially expensive to install. Nearly every patient who is admitted is going to need O2, even if it is just for a short period. Your architect also needs to understand the mission of hospice: It is not only about caring for the patients in the beds, but also for the family members who come to visit, and the engagement of the community.

Interview architects carefully before you make a selection because, otherwise, you may get a hospice facility that looks like a hospital. Your architect must be able to create an intimate, caring facility where people can spend their last days and be comforted by being there.

Find a reputable construction company that will work together with you. I would strongly recommend also hiring an experienced construction manager to be your representative in the process. Let that person manage the construction experience, because, generally, hospice leaders are not experts in construction. You need an advocate who understands your mission and is part of the fabric of your organization, but who can also speak the language of construction and architecture. Otherwise, you might end up with something that looks great on paper but doesn't serve the day-to-day needs of your patients or staff. Consider working with a consultant who is familiar with the needs of a facility like yours and who has worked with staffing patterns, and have that person look at your plans. That too can save you a lot of money in the long run.

You must be a licensed hospice to operate a hospice care center. That may sound obvious, but there are groups around the country who want to build a hospice facility and then expect to contract with hospices to put their patients there. Unless the hospice owns and operates the facility, some type of license governing the operation of the facility is necessary. If you want to build a hospice facility and accept Medicare reimbursement for GIP care, your hospice must be licensed and Medicare certified. Often I see not-for-profit hospitals that have been sold to for-profit systems, and the proceeds of the sale are put into a foundation. Sometimes, those foundations want to build a hospice facility and rent out the space to local hospice providers. You must have all the proper licenses to operate a hospice care center, and you must make sure to meet the requirements of your state and local laws. Some states require a certificate of need application before the hospice care center can be built. This is a key part of the due diligence process.

RAISING THE MONEY

Once you have done your feasibility study, you have identified a clear need, you're certain that the physicians and discharge planners will refer, and you've chosen an appropriate site, it is time to pull your funding together. We covered capital campaigns in general in a previous chapter, but having a capital campaign committee specifically directed to raise the money for the bricks and mortar of a hospice care center is essential. Make sure you have people on the committee who understand and enjoy fundraising and who are not afraid to ask for money or who have their own means and desire to give.

A hospice care center or hospice house can be an anchor for the hospice in the community, the place that gives the hospice a presence and that makes it clear that your hospice has invested in the community and vice versa. Anchors provide stability, but they can also drag you down. My most important piece of advice to someone who is building a hospice care center is to be extraordinarily careful about the person you hire to run the care center operation. That person will make or break the success of the facility. It should be someone with a drive to succeed and a deep understanding of doing the right things at the right time. It must be someone who can lead the team, and that means leading the physicians, the nurses, the aides, the chaplains, and the volunteers, and inspiring everyone to provide extraordinary care while making sure the financial guidelines are adhered to. The ideal candidate for this job would be an upbeat, customer-friendly nurse who has financial and discharge planning experience and has managed a floor in a hospital. The staff members will primarily be made up of nurses who want to know their leader understands their work.

The least bit of drift away from your productivity standards could mean financial losses. Thus, the leader of that facility must be someone who is not only an excellent clinician but understands finances too. That leader should also understand the urgency of filling those beds appropriately, and the necessity of staying on top of whether the patients are still eligible for the GIP level of care or need to be switched to a residential level of care or transferred out.

Hospice care center managers need to be personable. Often they are the first to meet with families, or talk with difficult physicians, or engage the community member who comes to look at the facility. Spending adequate time in your search and spending enough money to get the right person are crucial to the success of the facility.

There are other, alternative models of hospice facilities that don't require a stand-alone building. Many hospices have created dedicated hospice units within hospitals or skilled nursing facilities for hospice and palliative care patients. The hospice can lease the space, remodel it to be more homelike, provide all the staffing, and contract with the hospital for ancillary services such as security, housekeeping, food, and linen services.

There are advantages to creating a hospice unit within a health-care system. It is a much smoother transition for some patients to go from a standard hospital room into a hospice unit via an elevator ride instead of an ambulance ride. Hospice units within hospitals often can stay more full than stand-alone facilities. These units can result in being more financially successful than freestanding care centers. However, many patients and families do not want to be in a hospital and would rather be in a place that is more like home.

With leasing, you don't have the investment of bricks and mortar, and if for some reason those units don't succeed, you can end your lease. Leasing the space for your care center within another facility is the lower-risk model. There are other models in which you lease the beds from the hospital and/or nursing home, and you pay for each bed you lease. But be sure someone with expertise and experience in these kinds of contracts does your financial pro formas before you step into an agreement like that. Be sure any unit you might remodel within a hospital is in a newer, more vibrant part of a hospital. Older buildings that are not used for acute care, or whose outward appearance is dated, can be detrimental to the success of a hospice unit.

Some hospices have decided not to build in-patient facilities. Some decide to work with local community hospitals and nursing homes to place patients in what we call a scatter-bed approach rather than building a bricks-and-mortar hospice care center. There are some hospices that own assisted living facilities for frail seniors.

I have heard consultants say, "Whatever you do, don't build a hospice house because it is a financial drain." And, if you only look at the bottom line, it can be, but if you look at what it offers your community and what you want your organization to stand for, it can be the most wonderful thing a patient and family can experience, mine included.

My brother had hospice care for the last four months of his life, and my mother took care of him until it became impossible for her. So Michael was admitted to the Halifax Hospice of Volusia and Flagler Care Center in Florida. They called me to say he had been admitted. "We are so privileged to have him here," they said. "He's comfortable, music is playing softly, the chaplain has come by and shared a prayer, and he's smiling." My dear brother died before I could arrive to see him, but knowing that he was cared for by these loving people for even one day in their facility was something that still warms my heart.

Fast-forward 18 years when my mother was in the hospital in intensive care with a massive stroke. Fortunately, the hospice that took care of my brother was still there to take care of my mother. And when she was admitted to the care center unit within the hospital, the chaplain came in and said, "It's such a privilege to have your mother here," not realizing that 18 years earlier, they had used the same words to me about my brother. Having a hospice facility with professional staff that provides compassionate care is meaningful beyond any bottom line gain. I still have people thanking me for having built the hospice care center in Gainesville 20 years ago. You cannot put a price on that.

Remember you must have a strong business plan to survive. Weigh all of your options before you build, and if you decide to go forward, do it with gusto and commitment and the belief that you will succeed. Have the right person in charge, and you *will* succeed and you will make a difference in people's lives.

In Conclusion

"This above all: to thine own self be true; And it must follow, as the night the day; Thou canst not then be false to any man."

—WILLIAM SHAKESPEARE

What do I hope to have accomplished with this book? It has been written as a reminder to readers to stay true to the original mission of hospice: human care of body, mind, and spirit. Have the courage to incorporate your values and wisdom, courage and kindness, and indeed, even love into your work. I am living proof that if you do those things, you can be successful.

We should never forget that hospice care started out as a social movement and an alternative to traditional care, though it has long since become an accepted part of the health-care experience. Still, hospice is so much more than a health-care product; modern-day hospice is a reflection of those ancient hospices, way-stations for weary travelers. Today's travelers are on their final journey and we have the privilege to stand with them, encouraging, supporting, uplifting, soothing, and loving them on their final journey from this life. We care for the frailest of the frail who need not only relief for their suffering bodies but also comfort for their hearts, minds, and spirits. That is our charge and it is so much larger than simply health care.

Remember to care for your patients and families, one person and one family at a time. It is their journey, not yours. Your job is to give them whatever they need to make their own decisions about how they want to live out their lives.

Always keep the focus on your mission, your guiding star and your reason for being. Stay true to yourself and the reason you are in this work. Be brave enough to take your blinders off from time to time. Instead of saying, "We've always done it this way and we don't need to change," look for the third way, the new path. Don't fear change; embrace it and always hold to the original principles of hospice care: dignity, respect, choice, and empowerment.

Love what you do. Take your work seriously and take yourself lightly. Above all, *care*. Care about yourself first. Then care about the staff and the volunteers who give themselves to this work. Then care for your dying patients and their family members, those brilliant teachers who allow us into their lives, and from whom we learn every day.

And finally, remember you must have a mission, and you must also have a margin. By focusing on both you will thrive.

CPSIA information can be obtained at www.ICGtesting.com
Printed in the USA
LVOW04s0510211014

409635LV00003B/4/P